This Book Belongs To

SAMPLE DESIGN

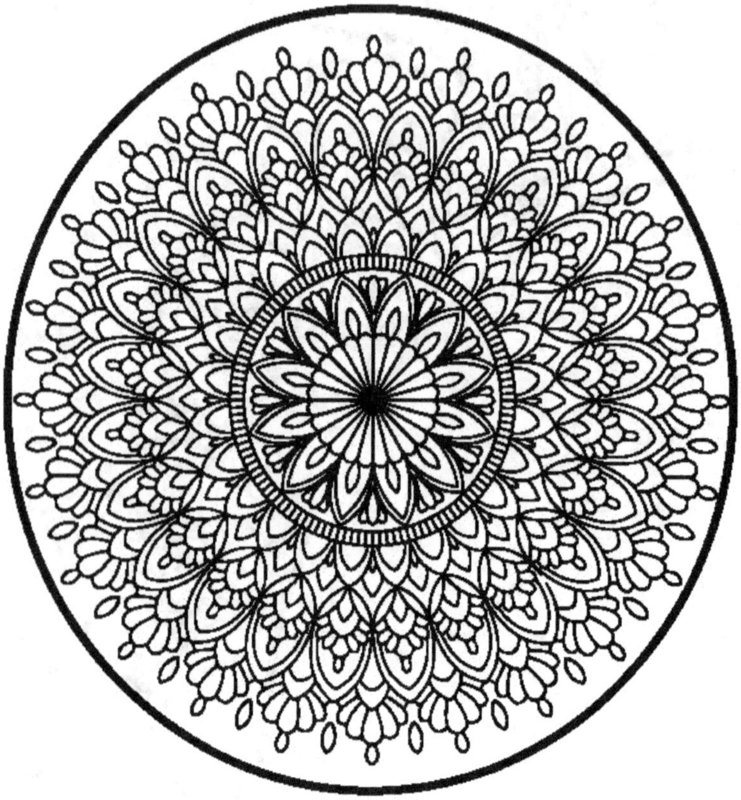

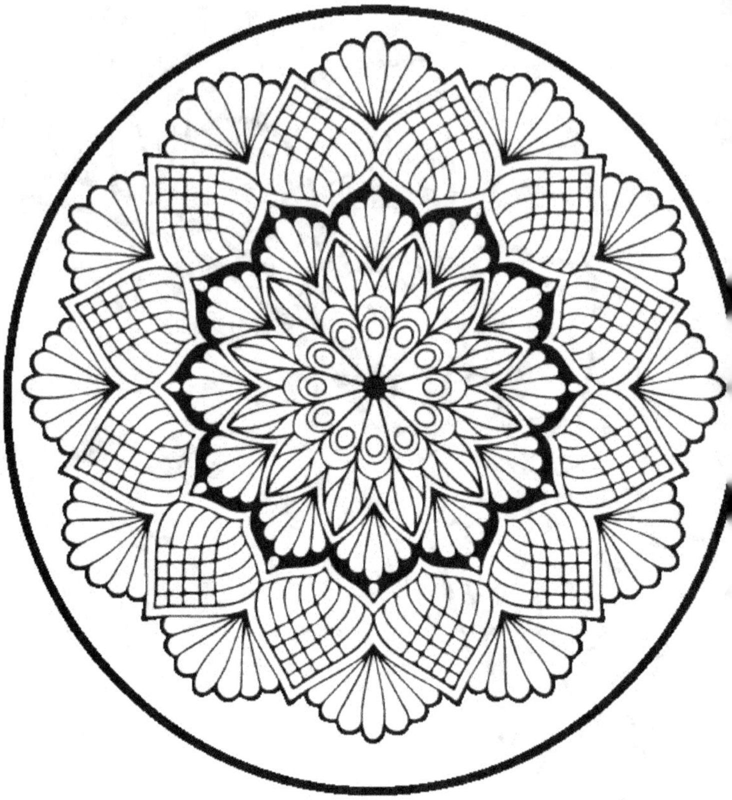

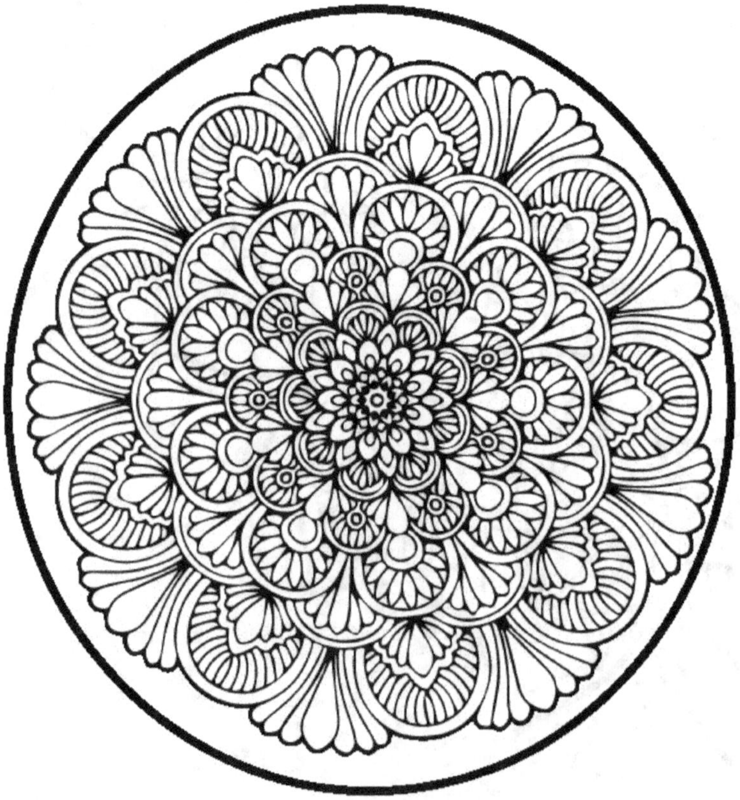

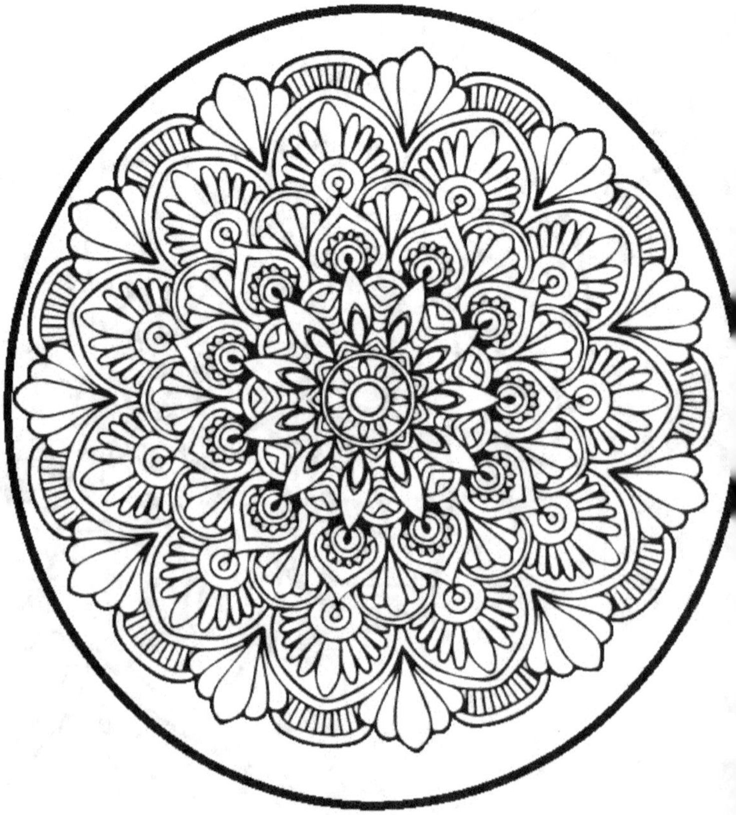

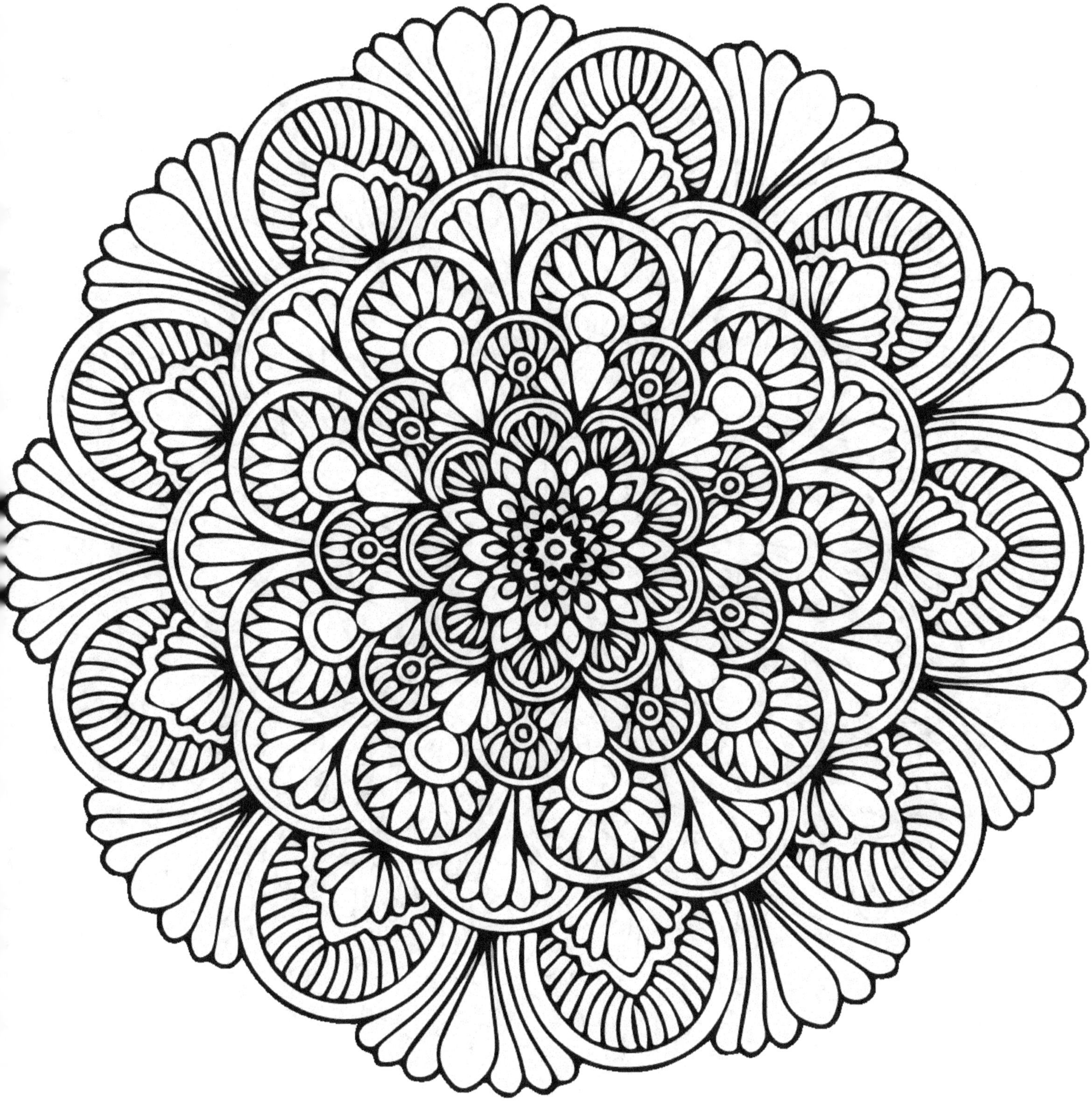

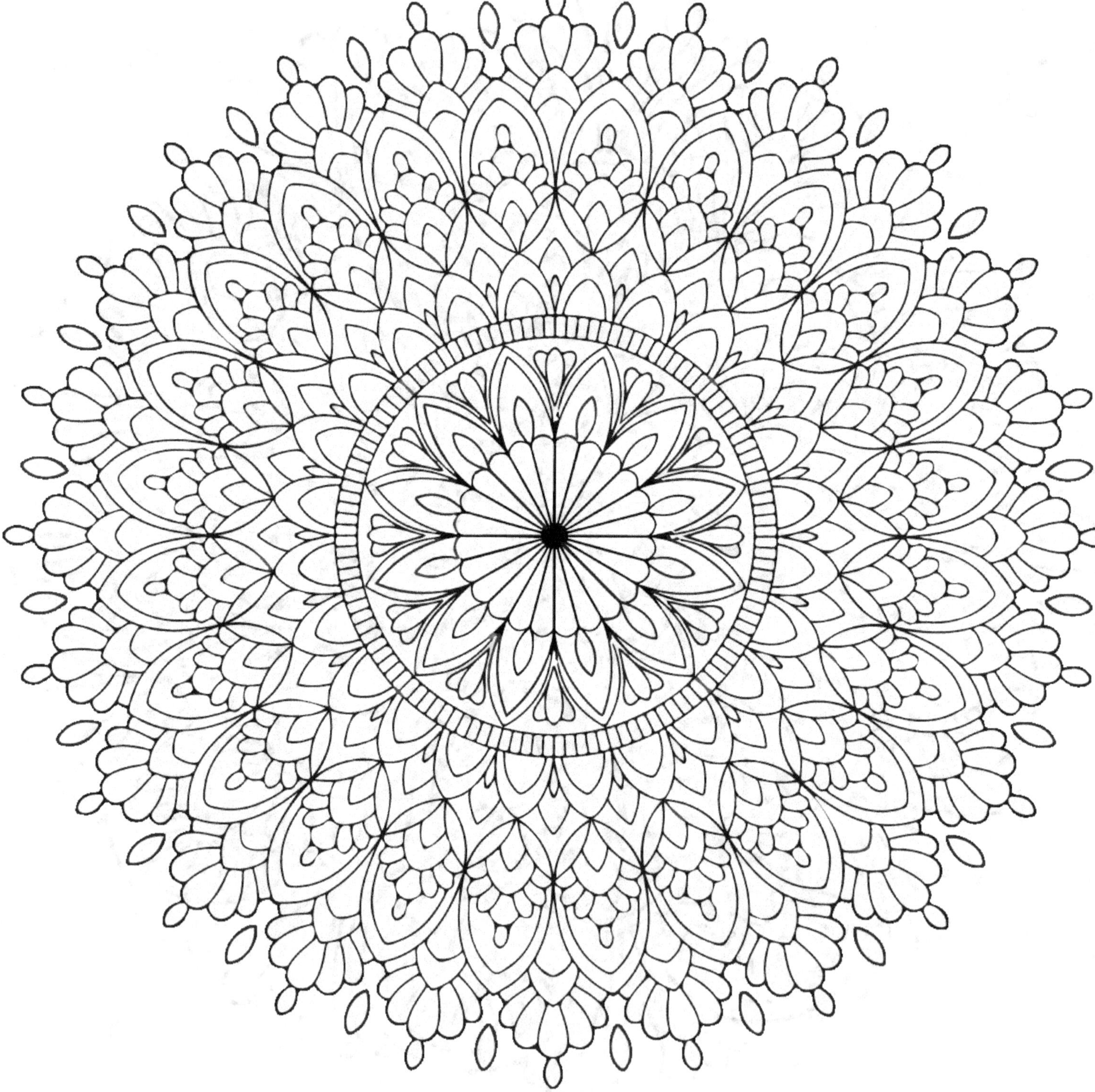

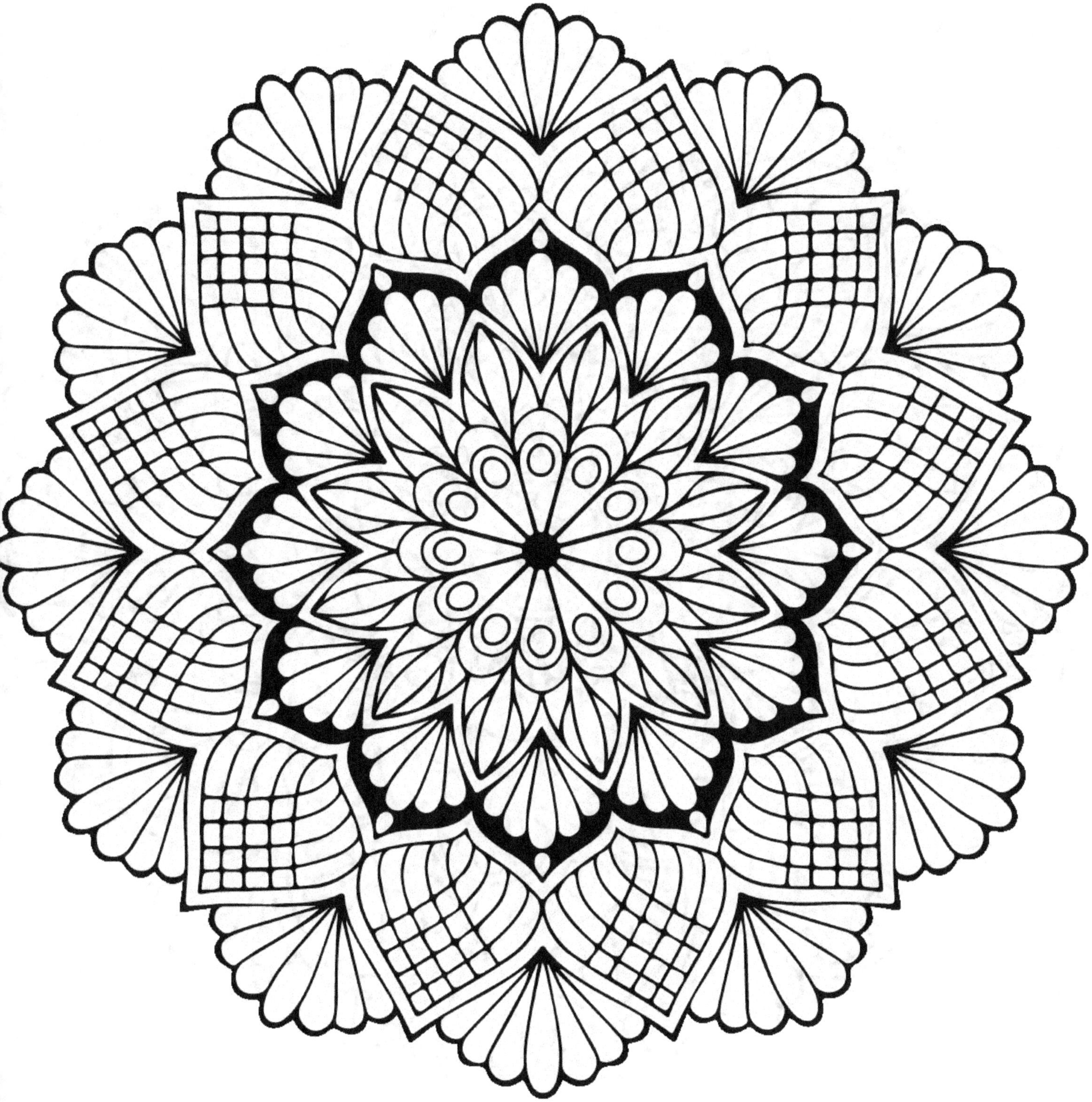

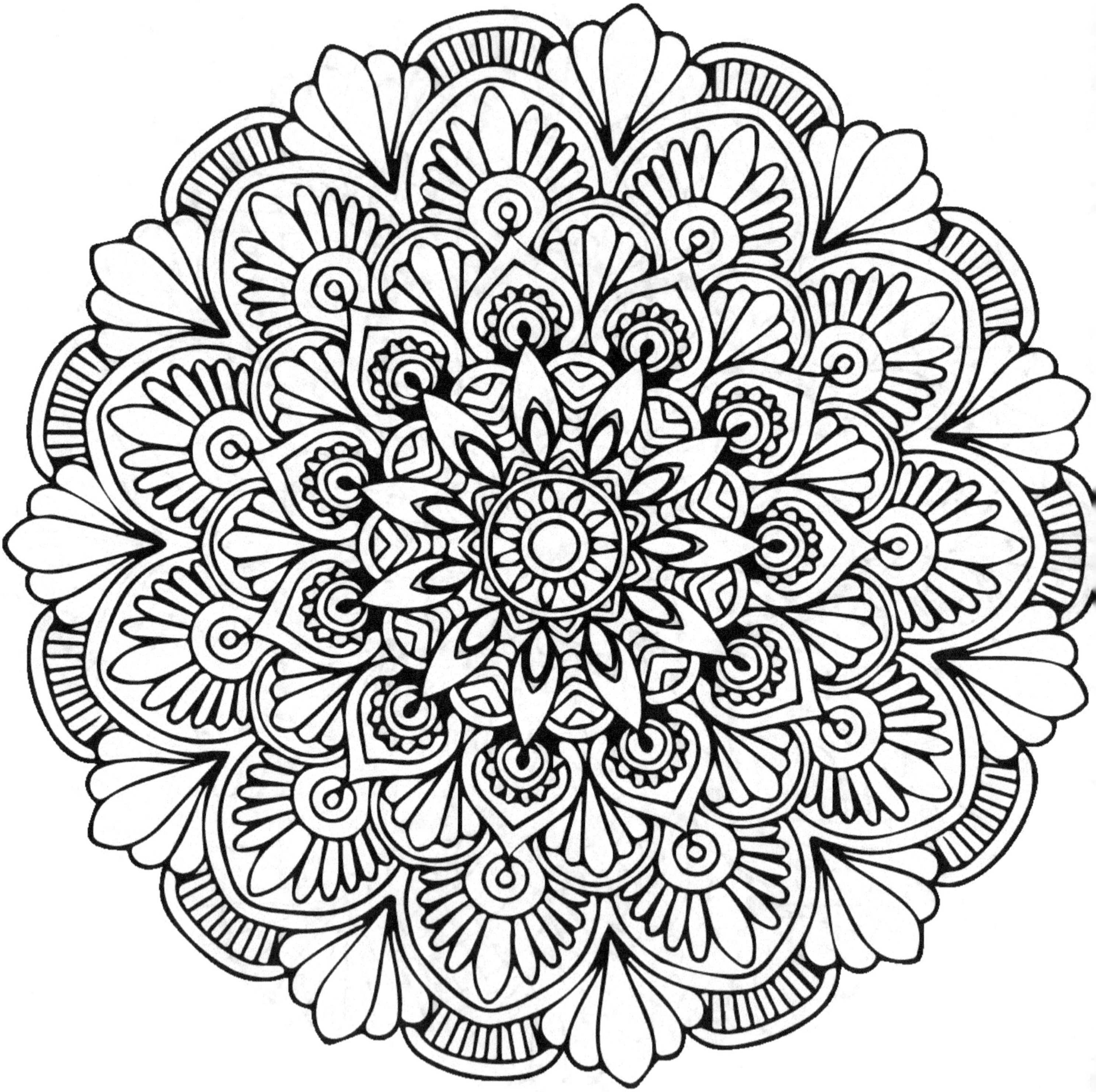

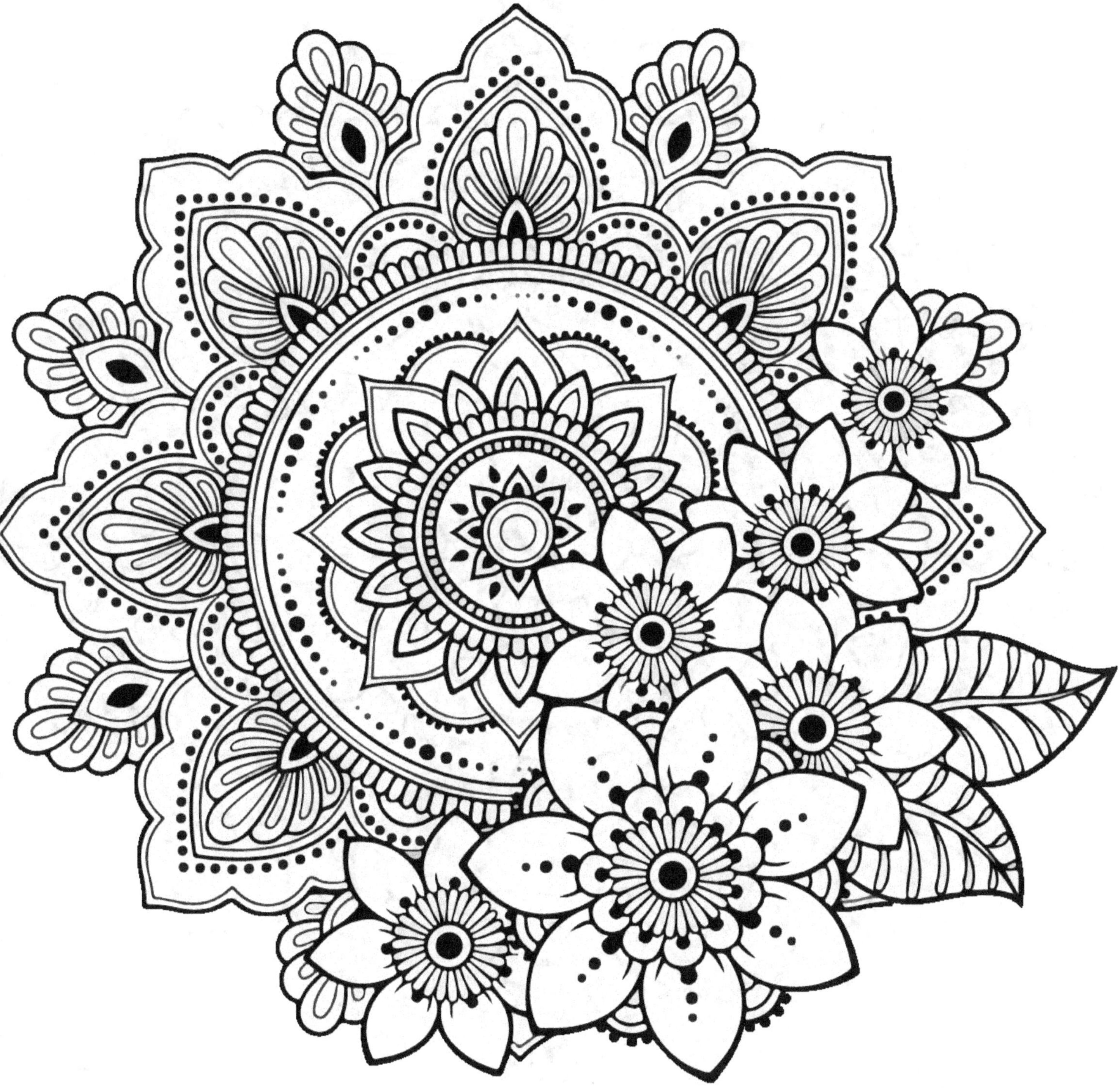

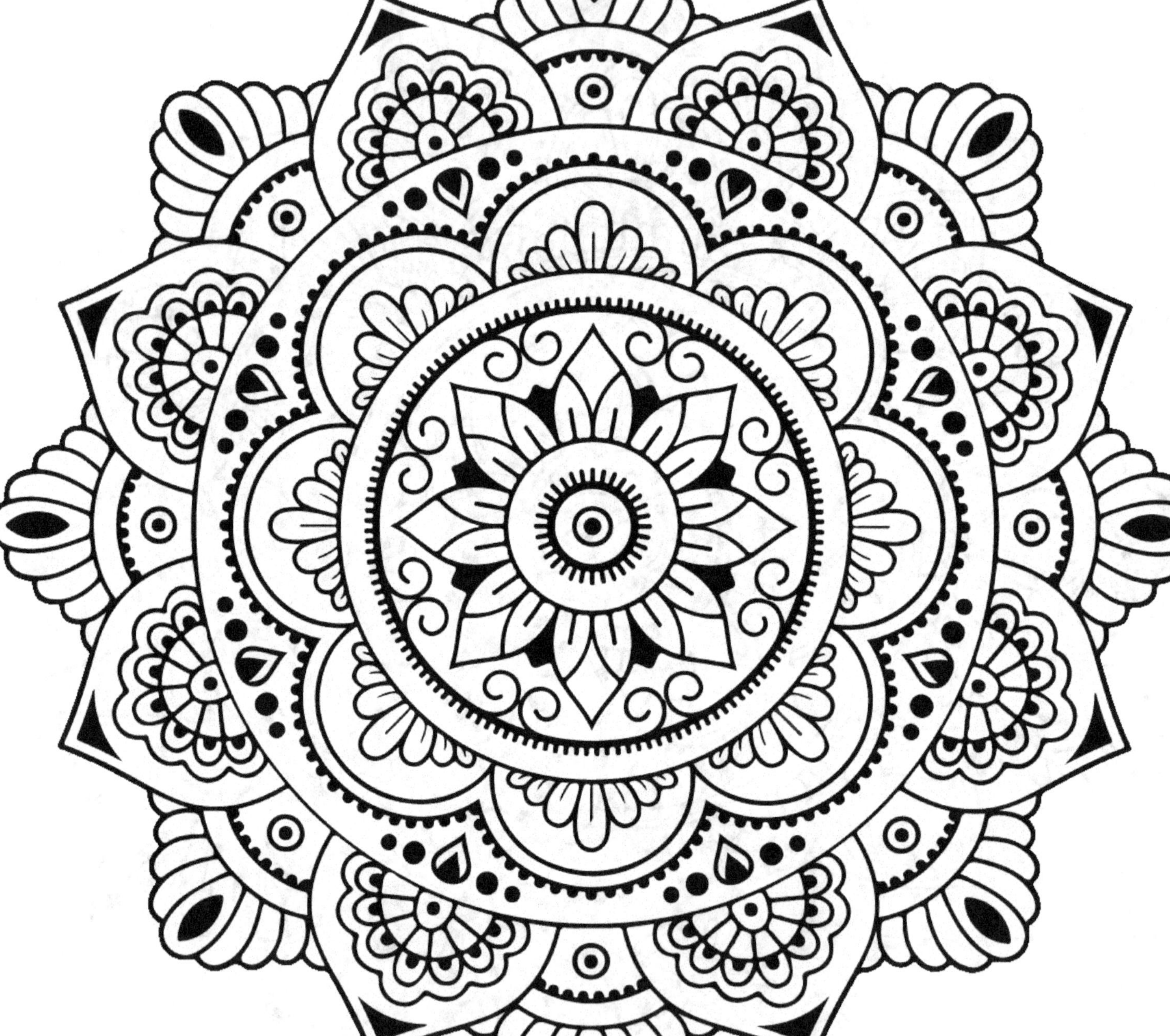

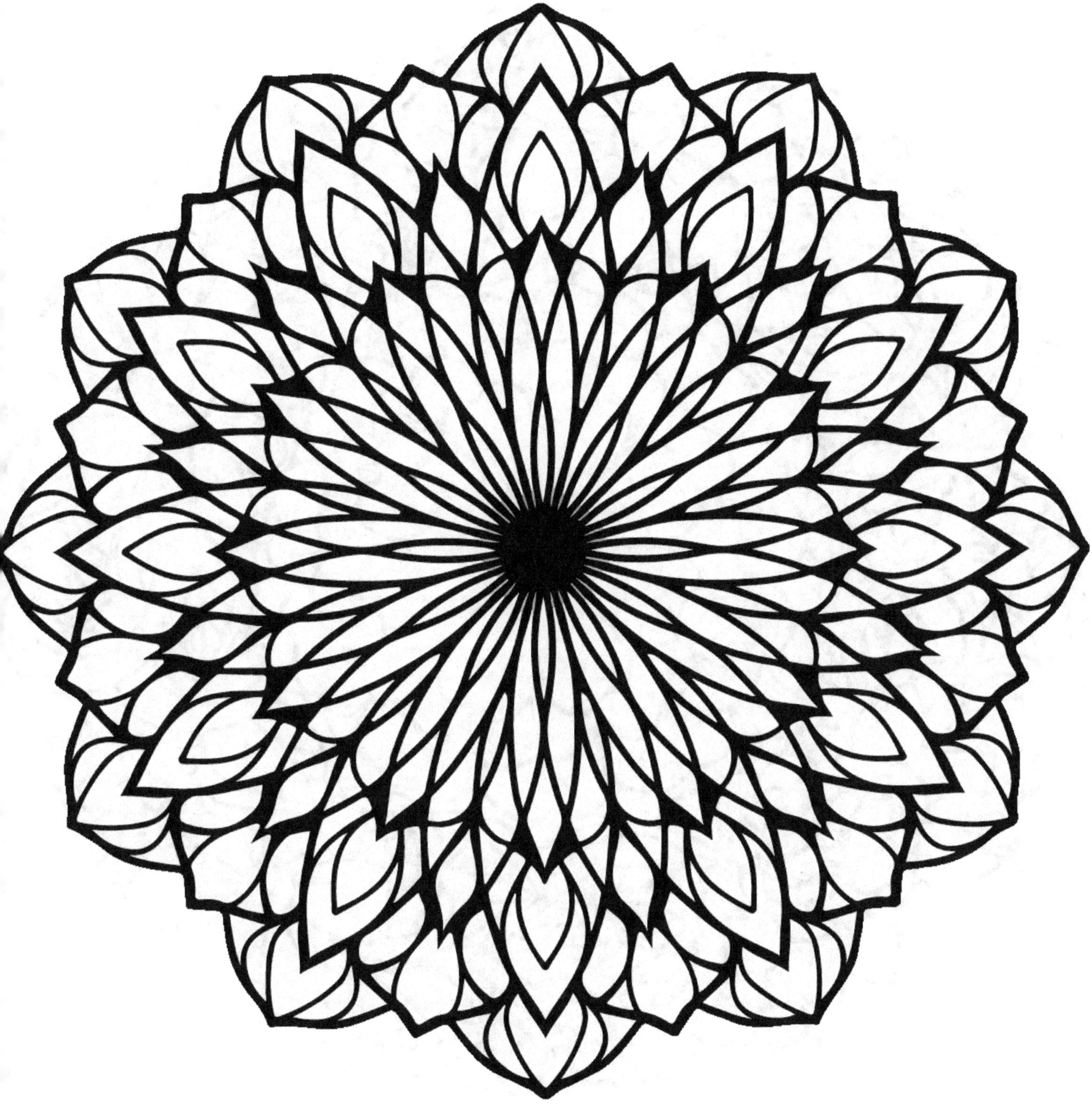

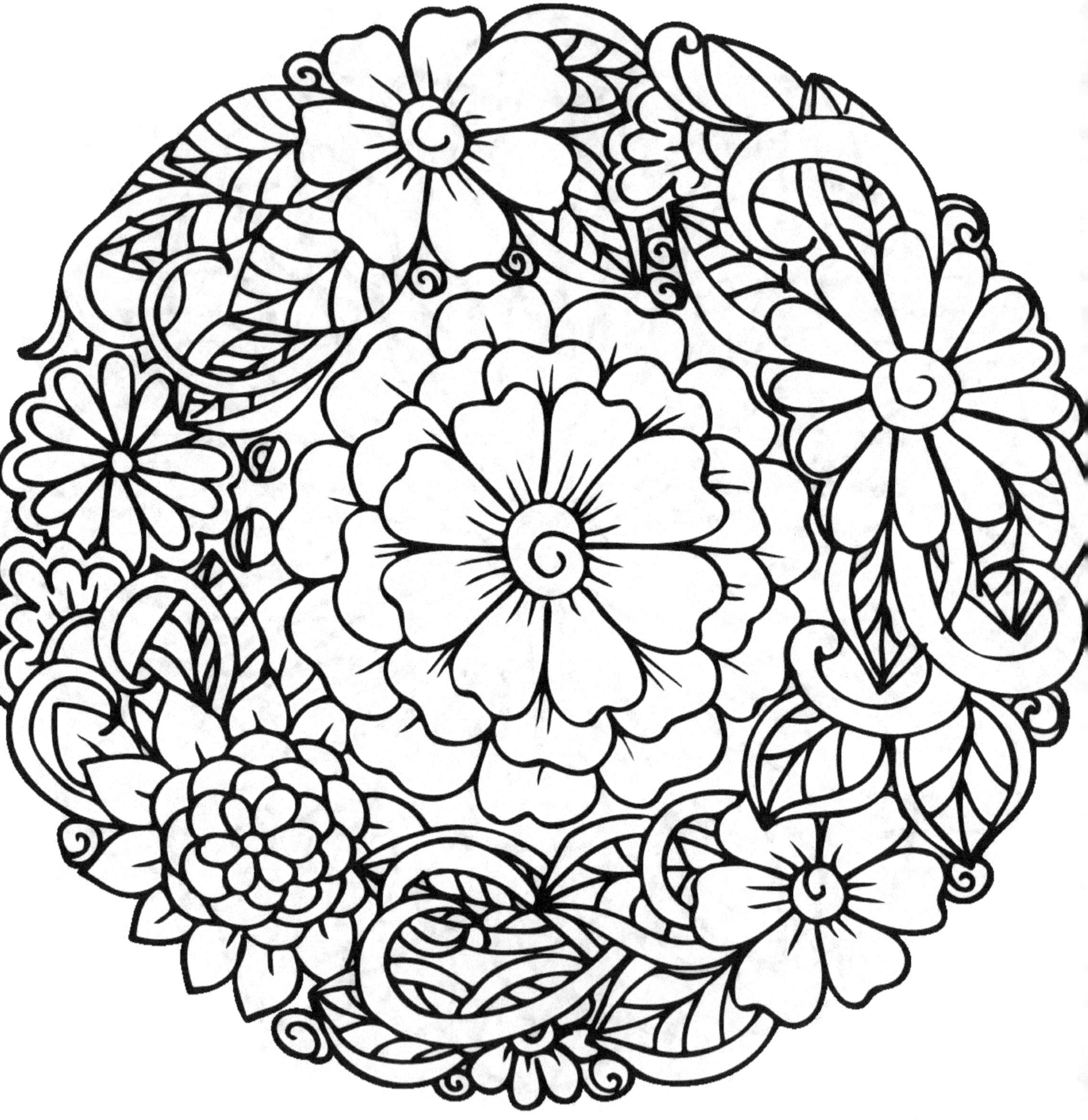

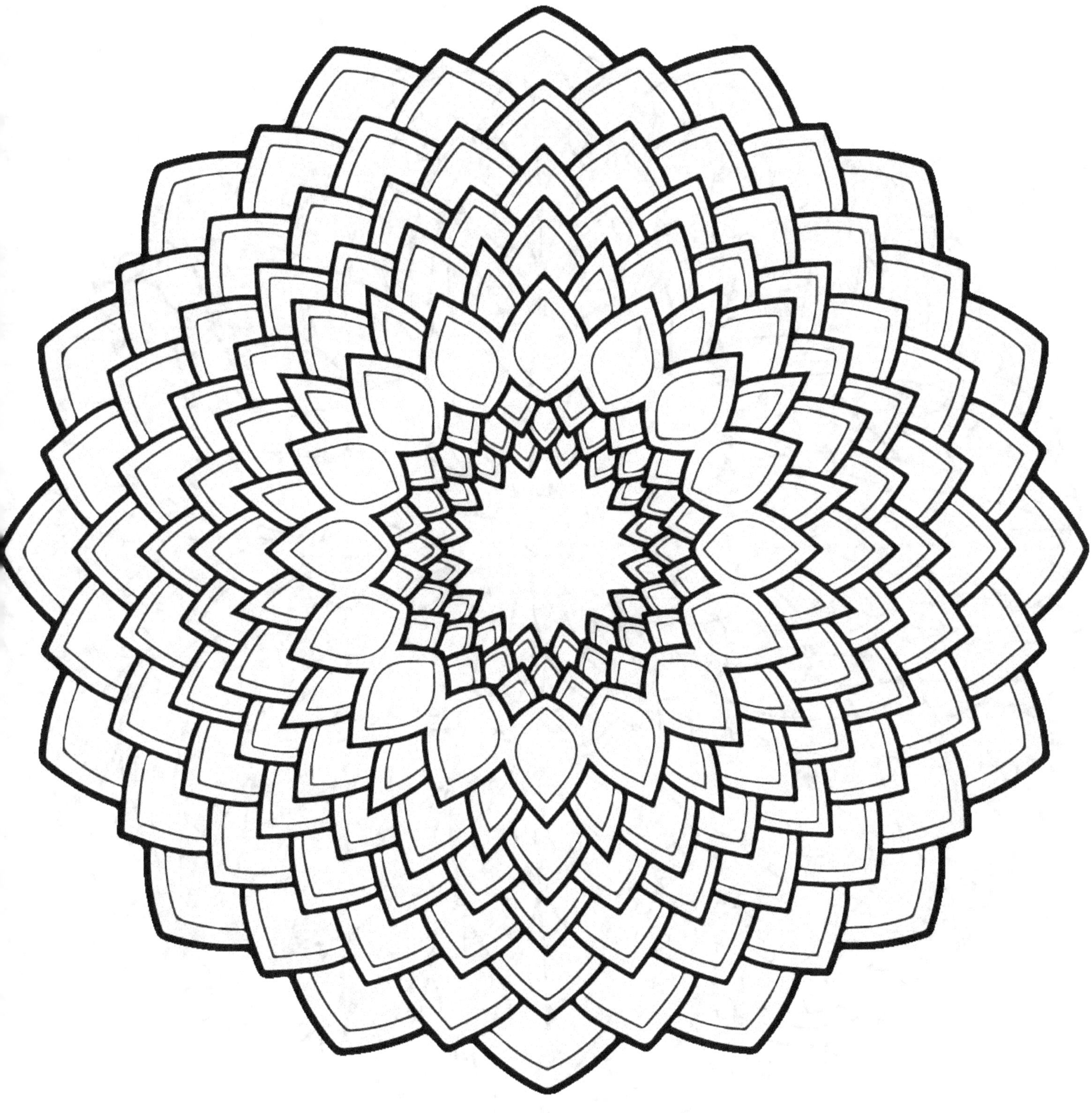

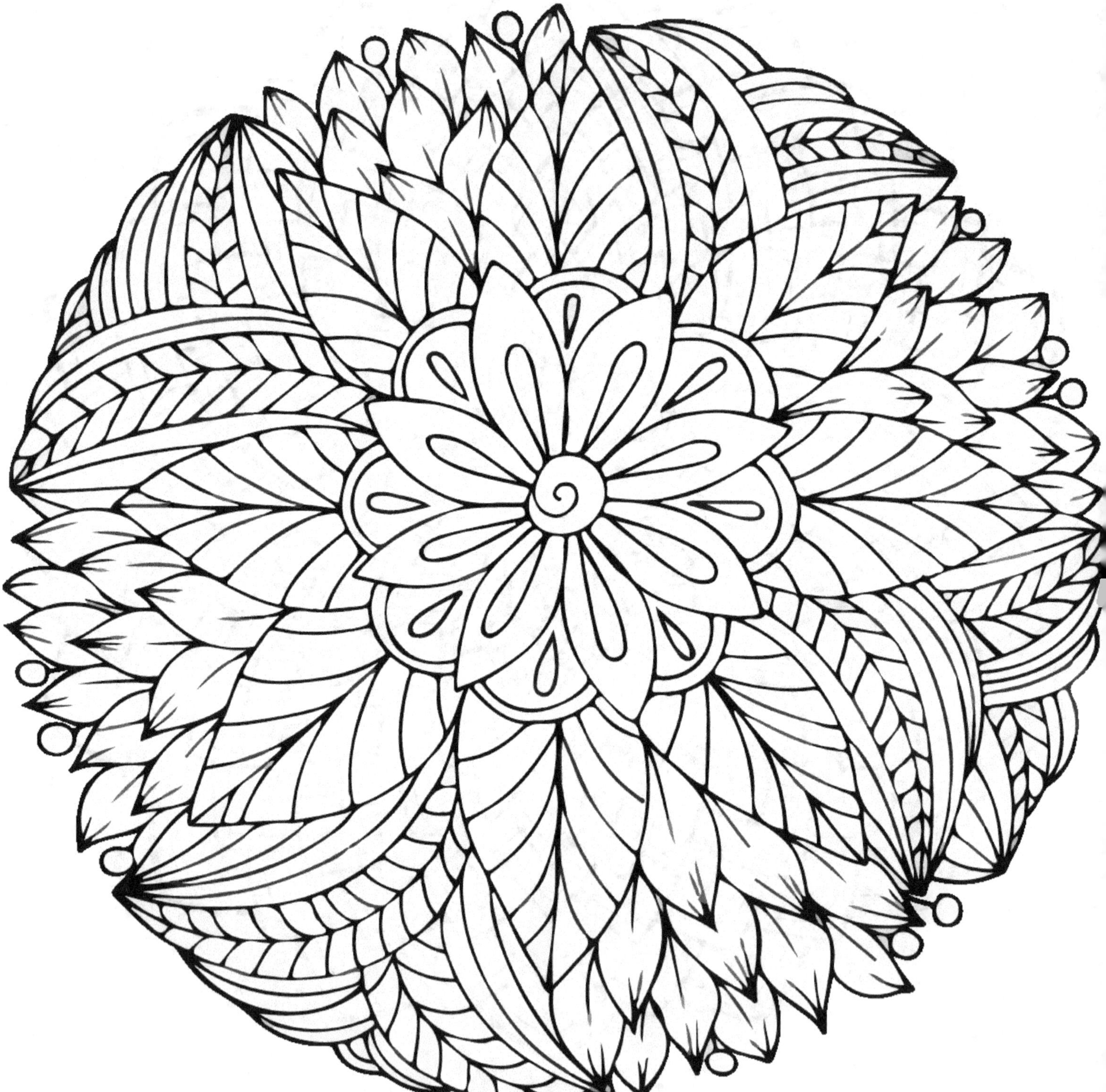

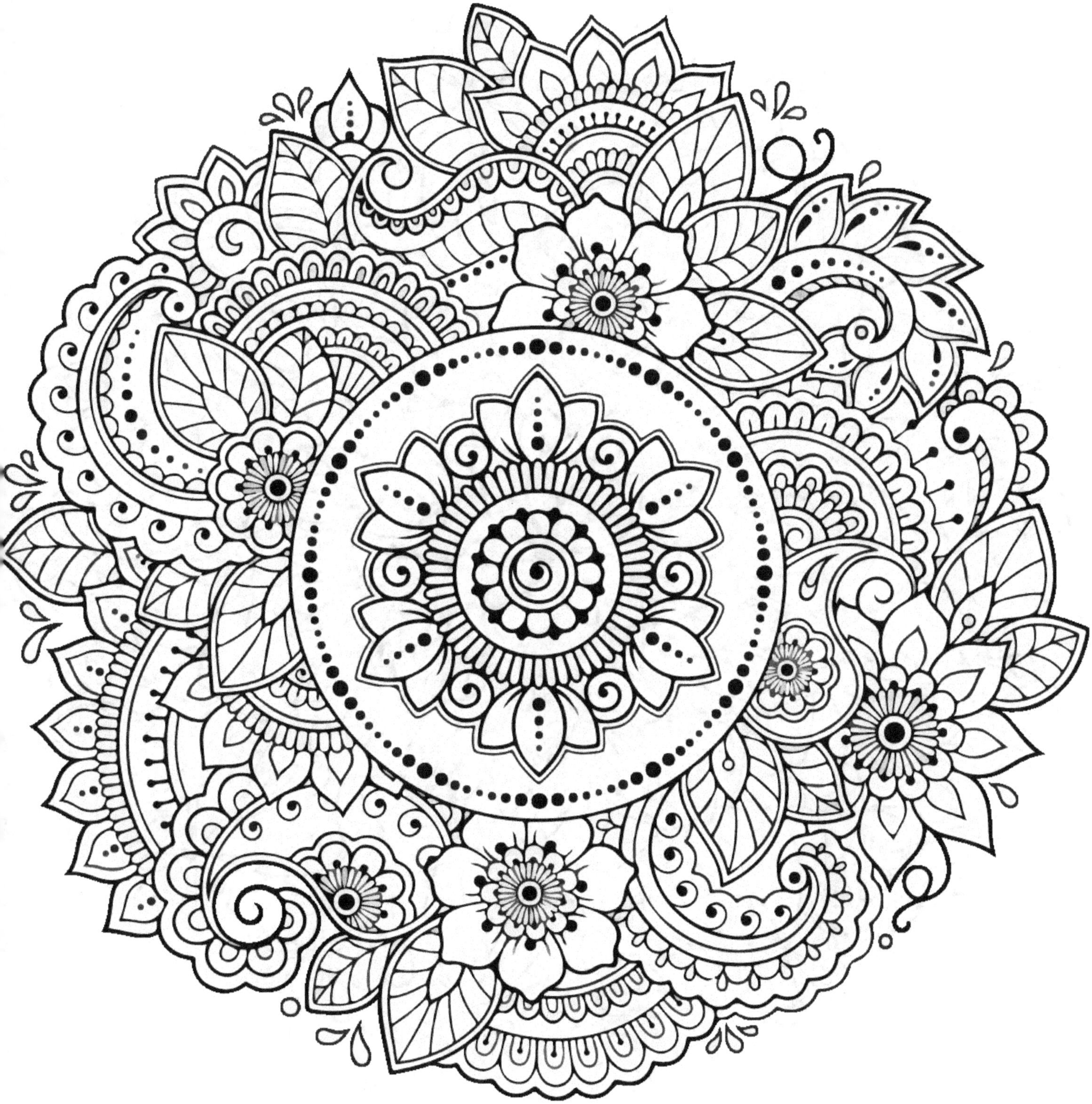

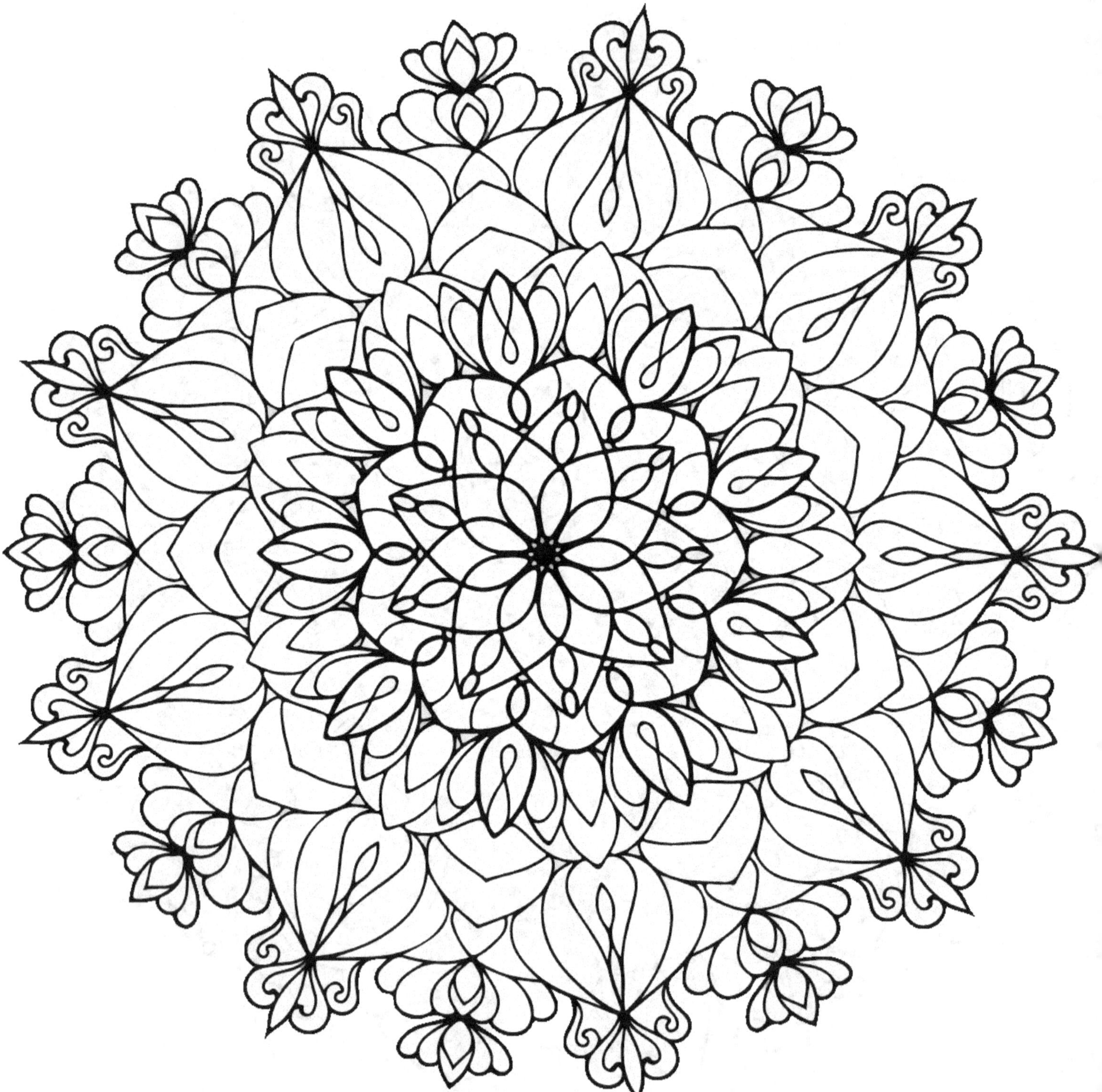

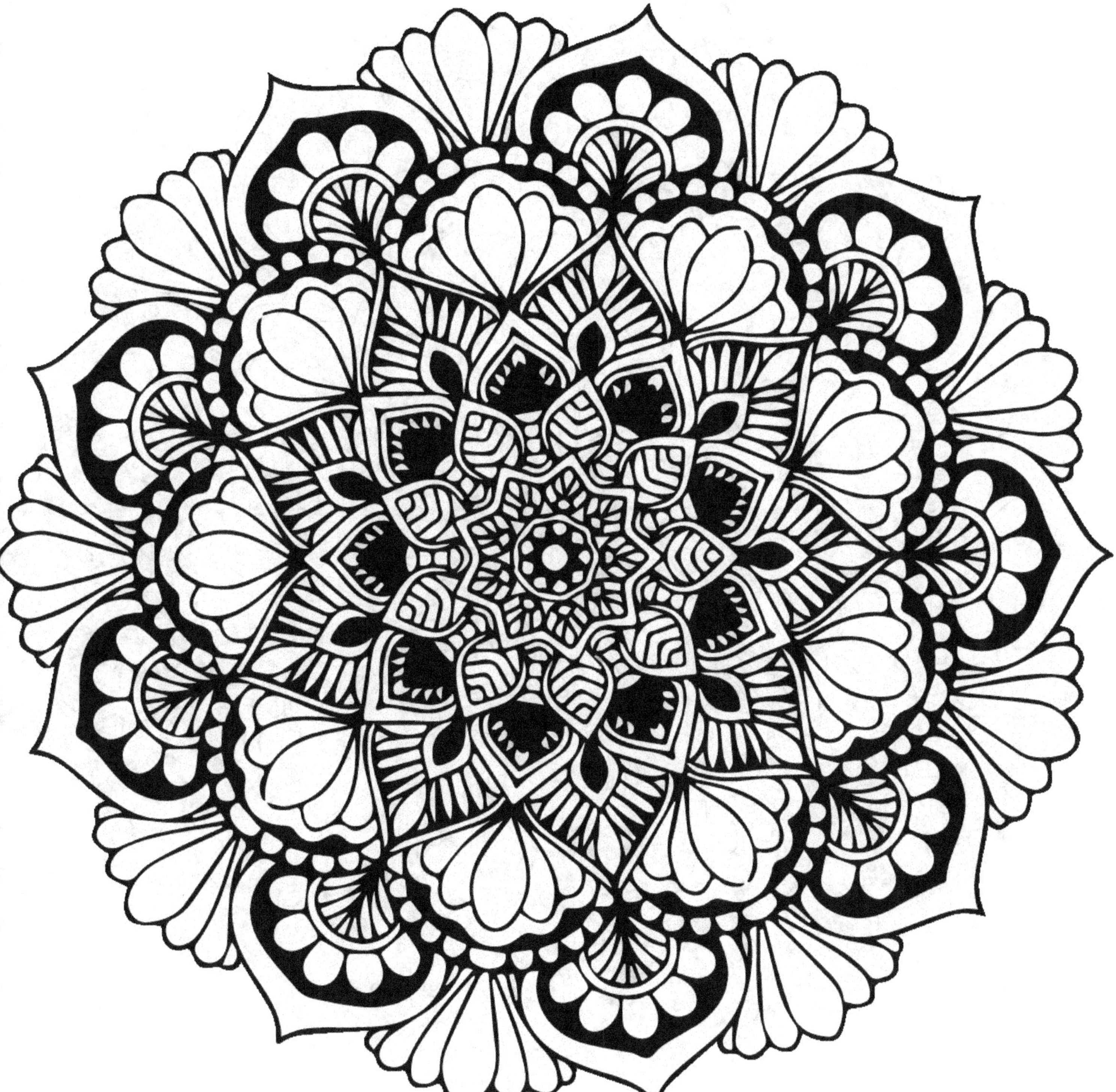

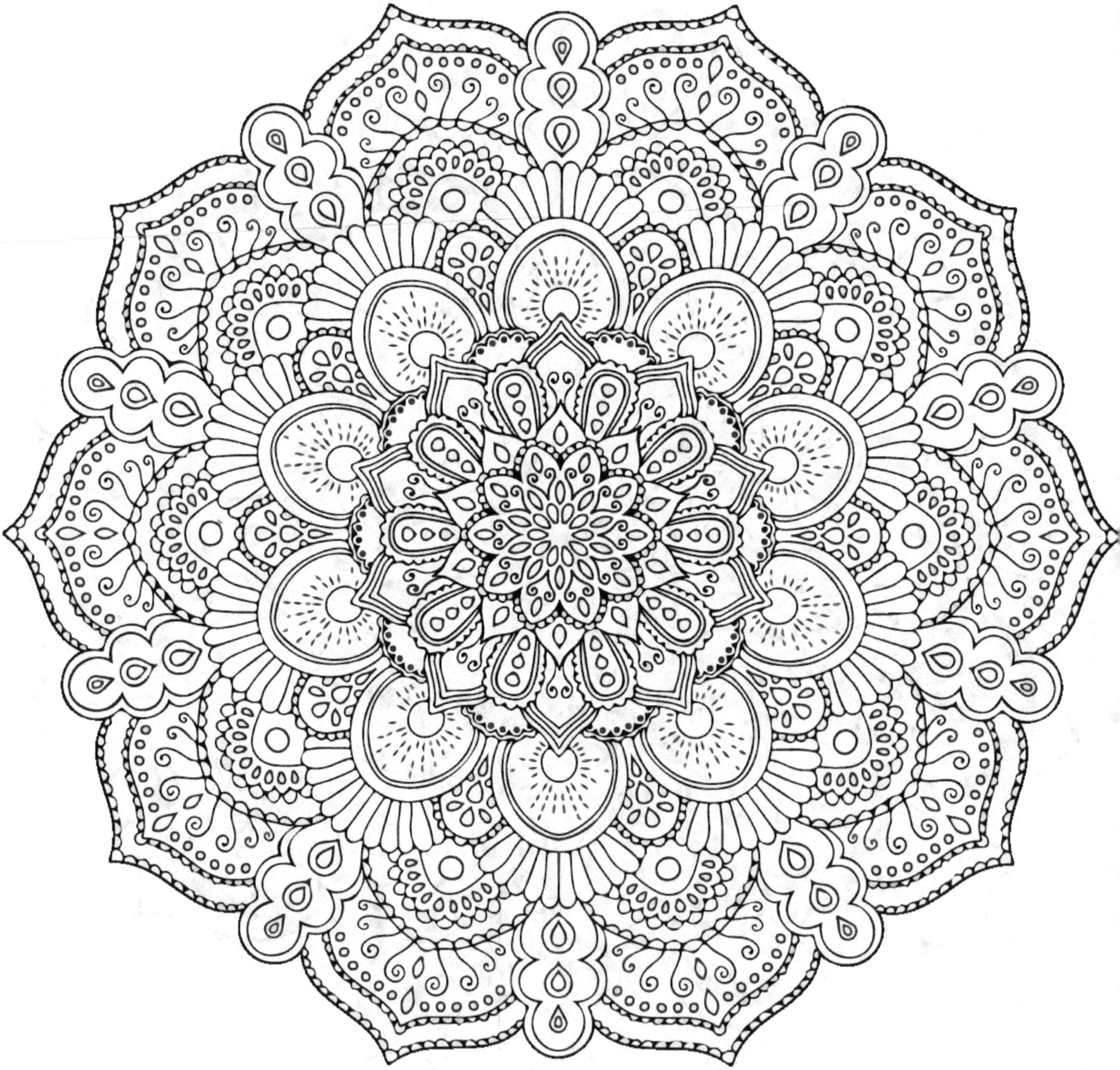

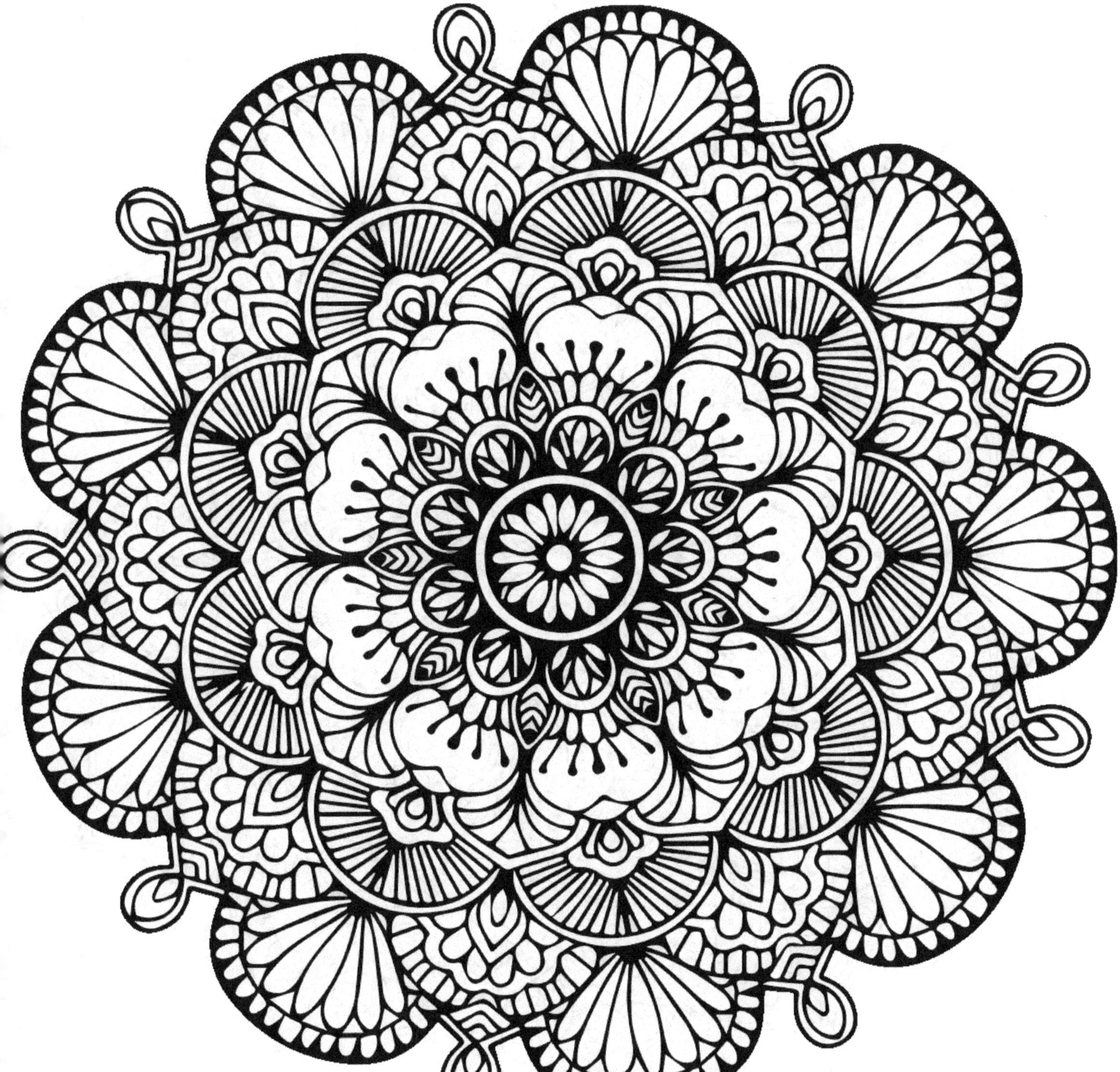

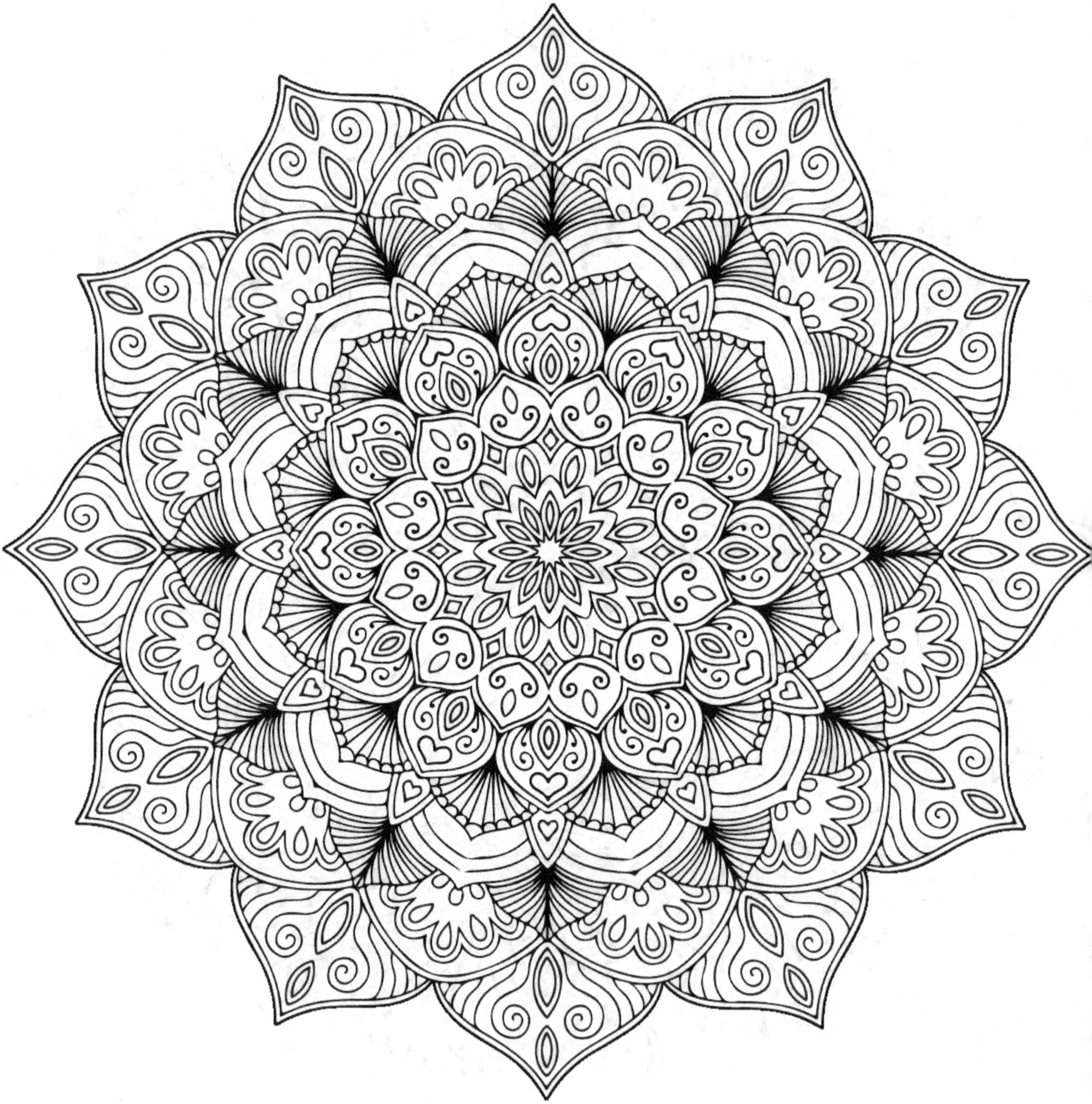

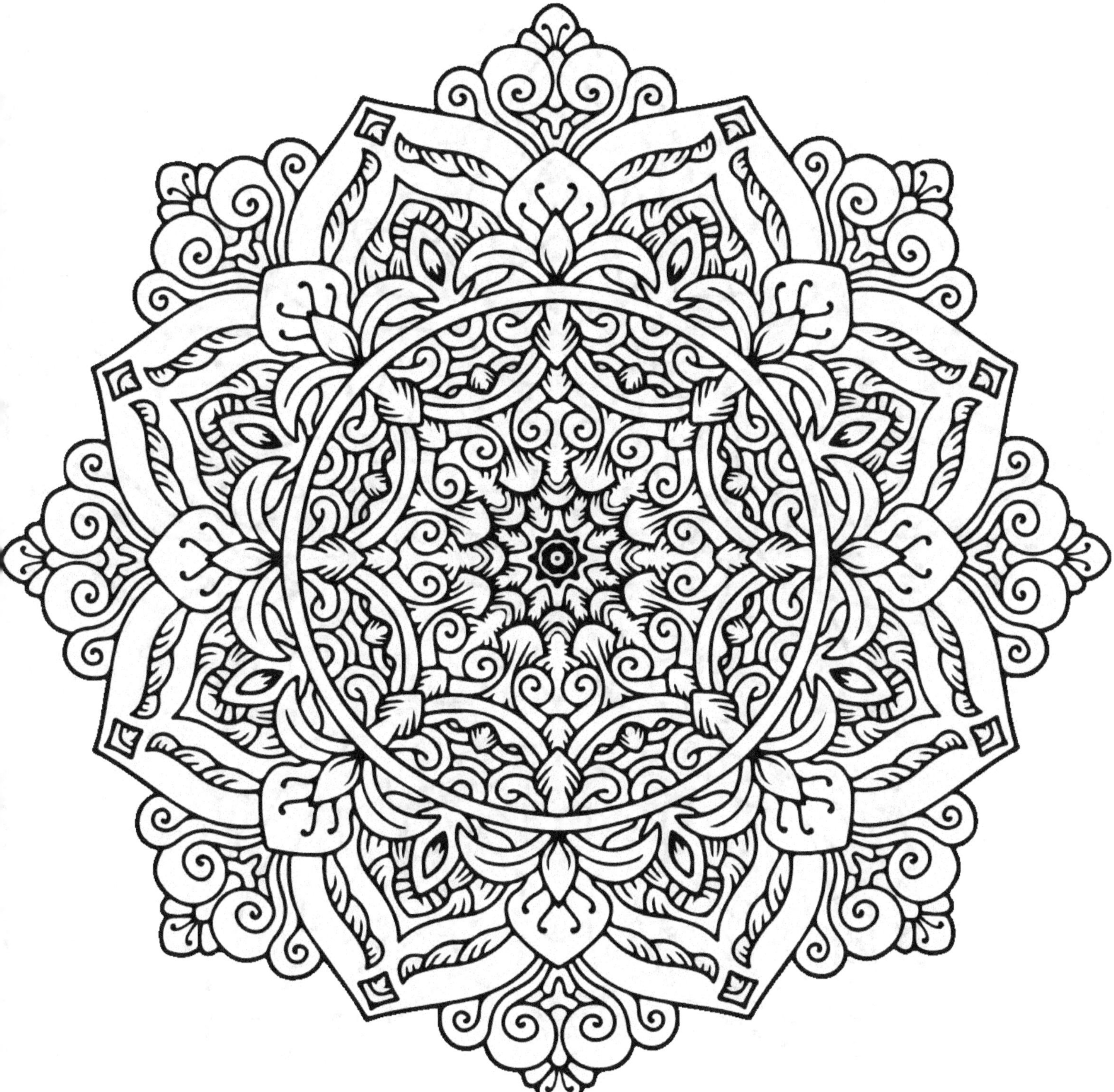

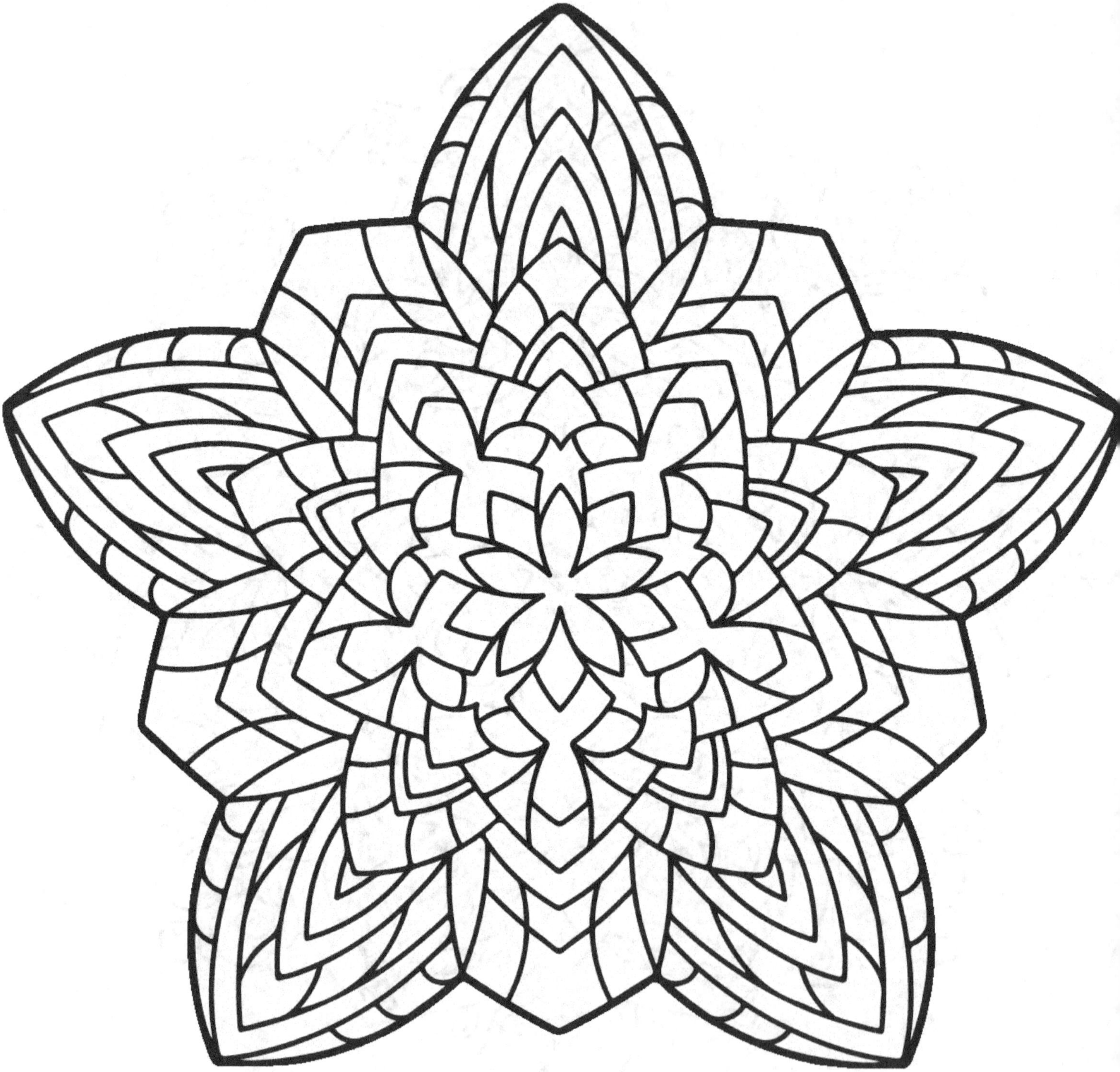

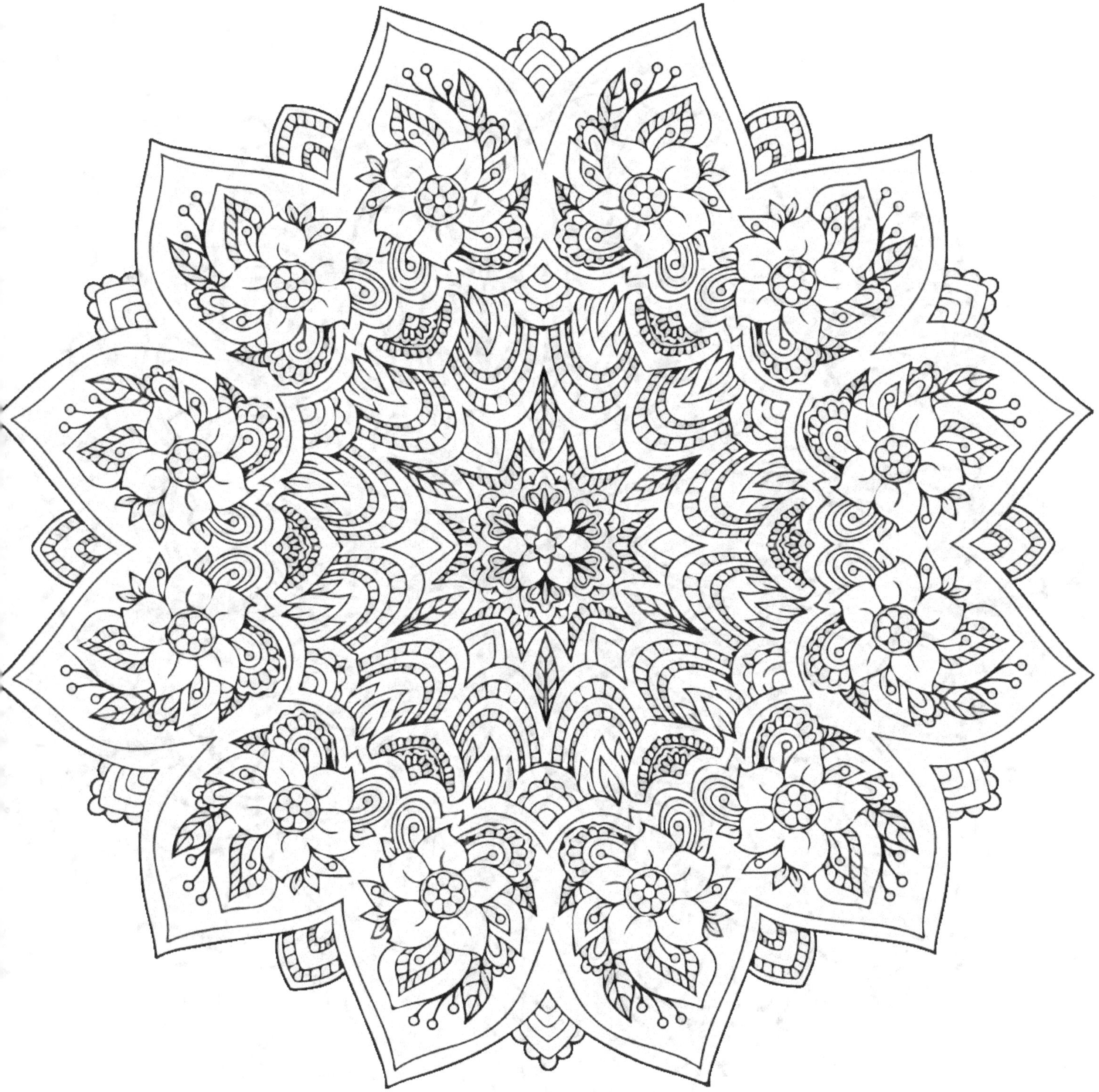

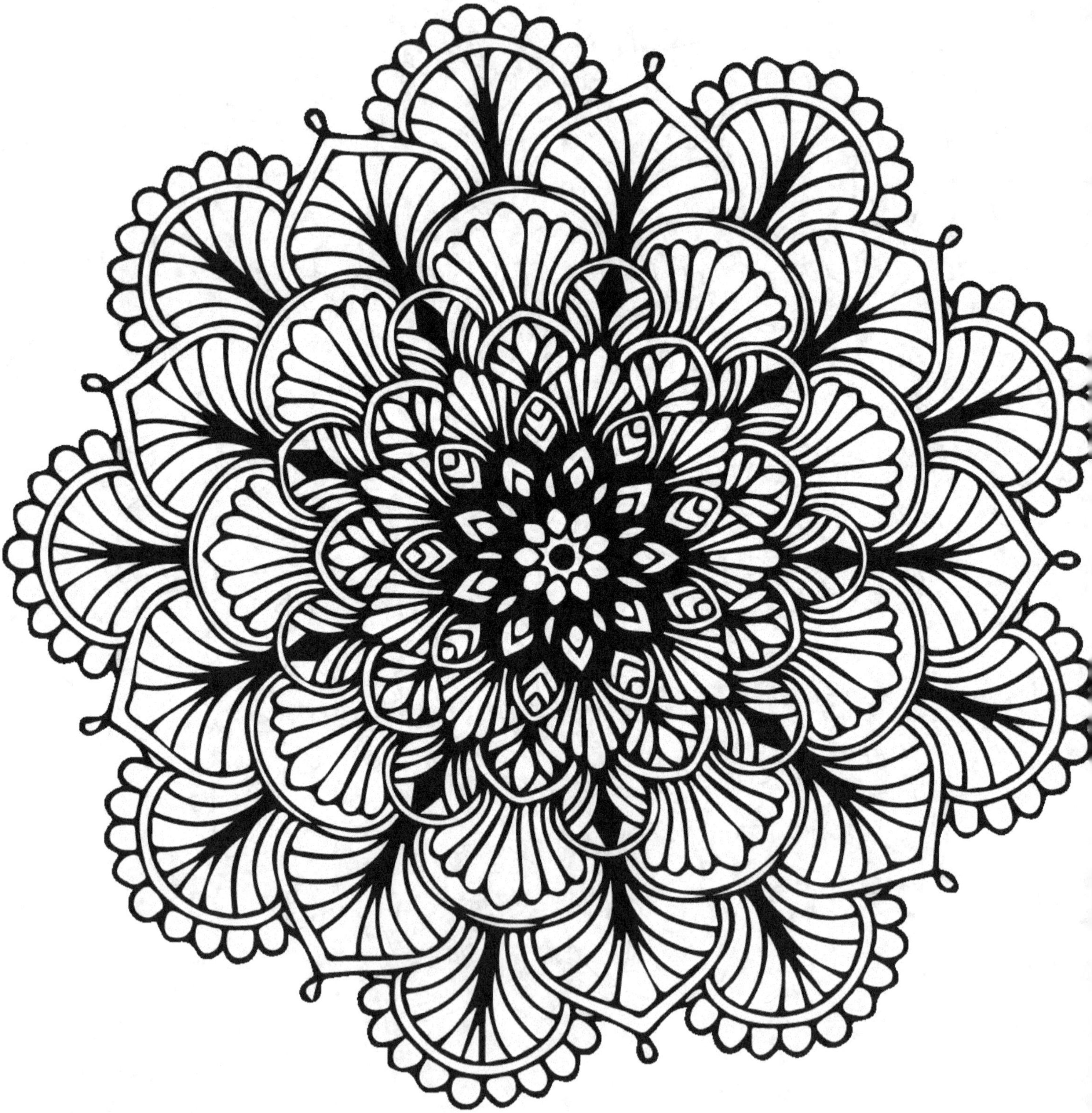

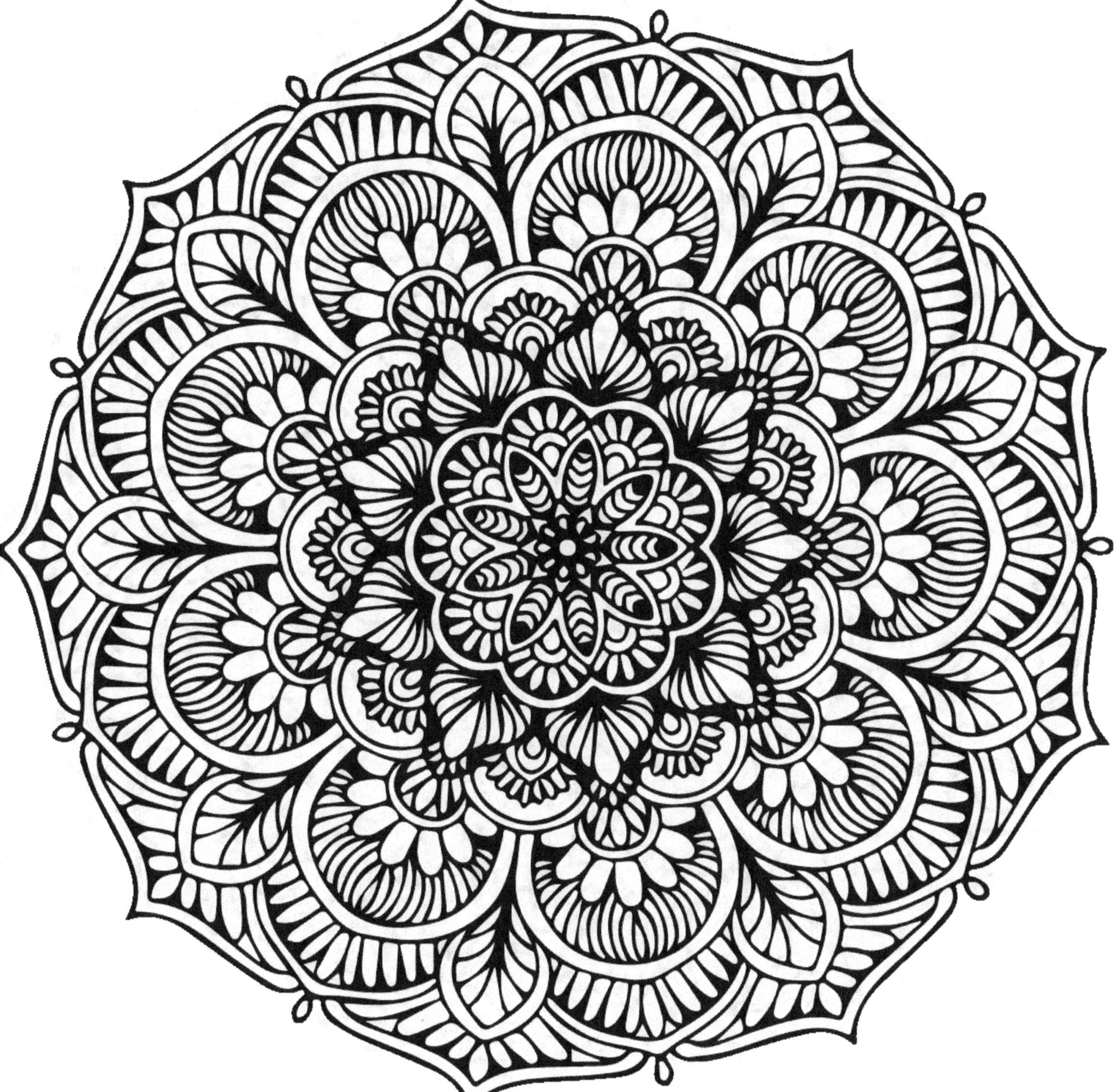

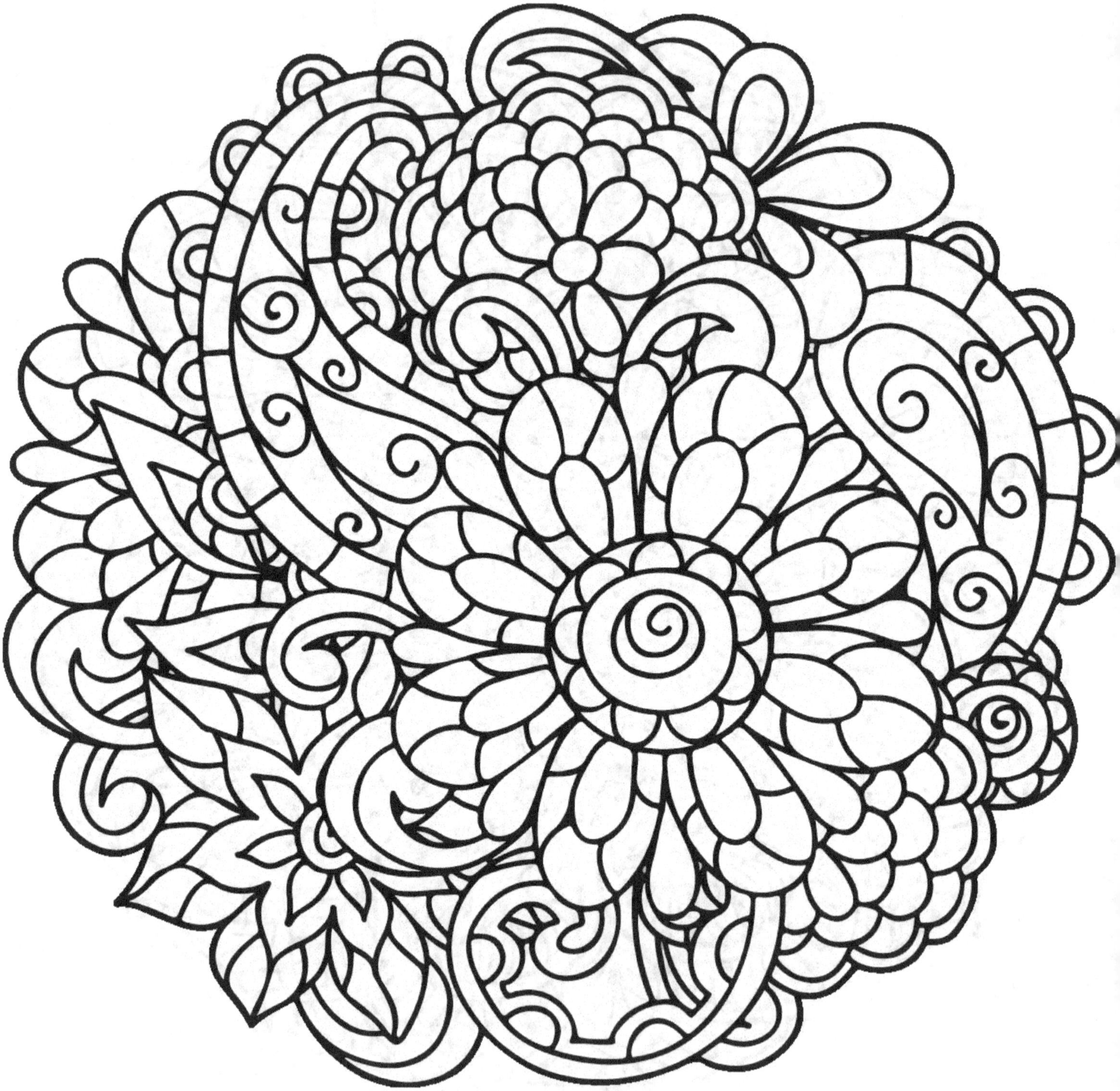

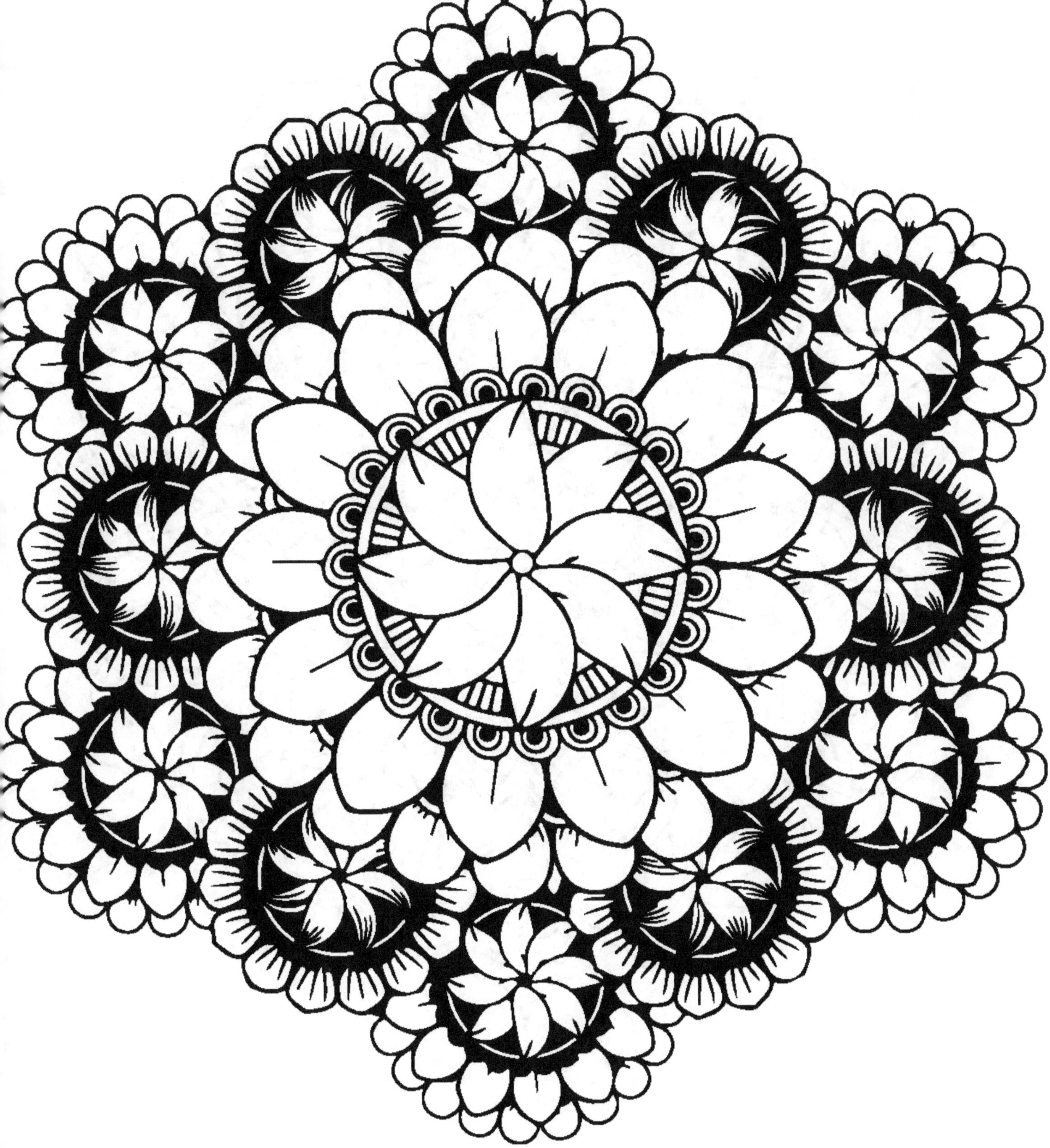

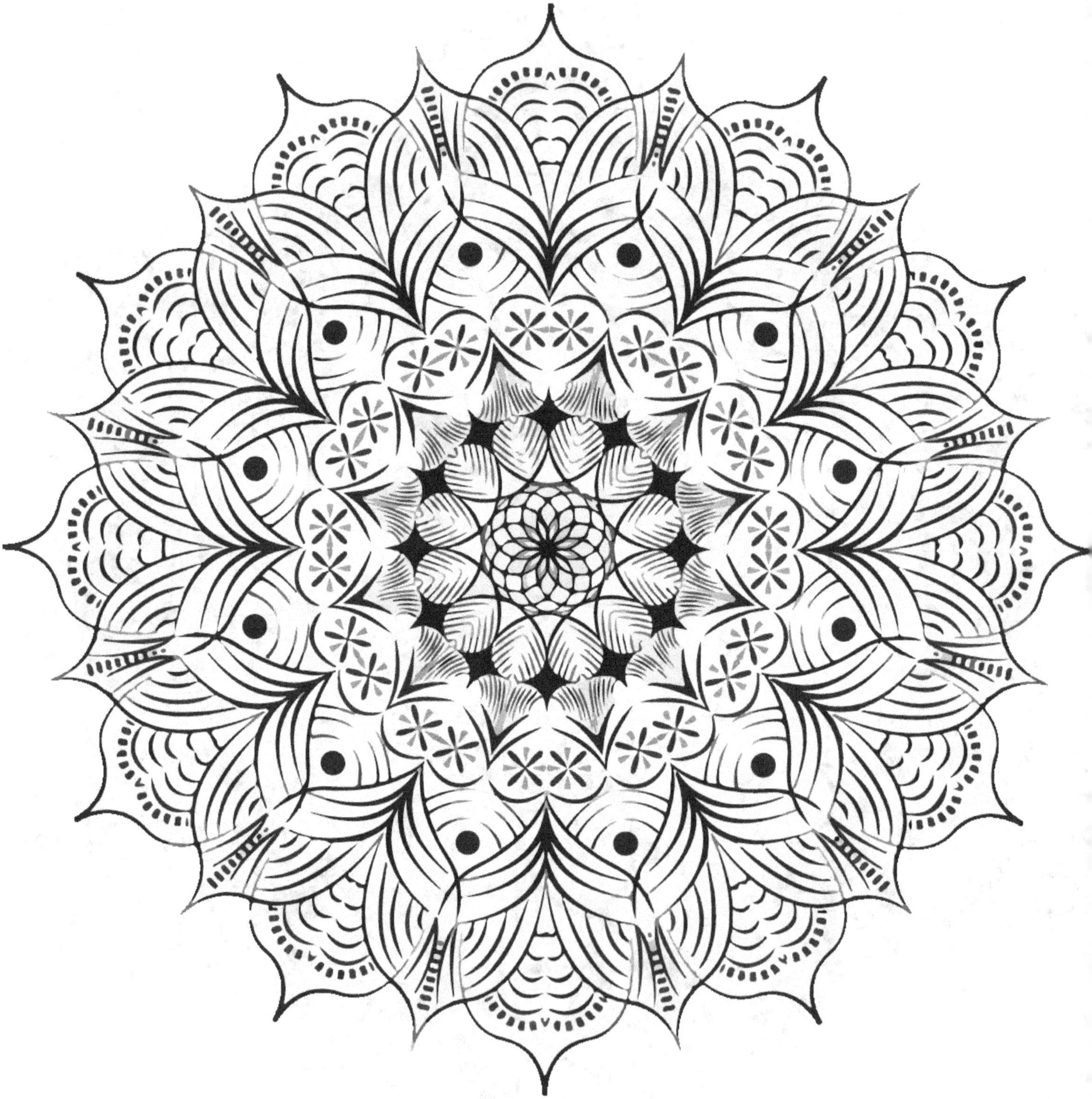

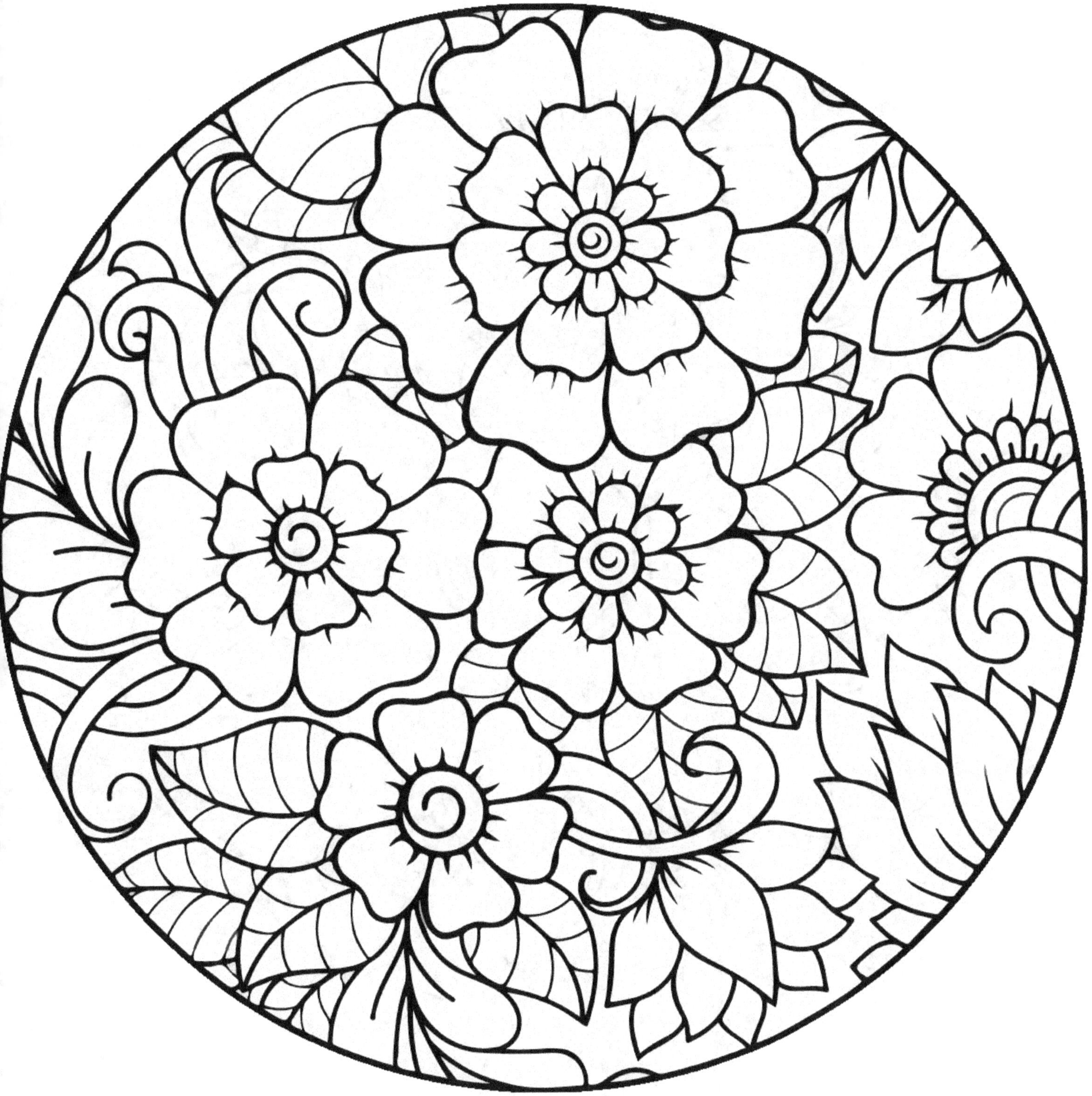

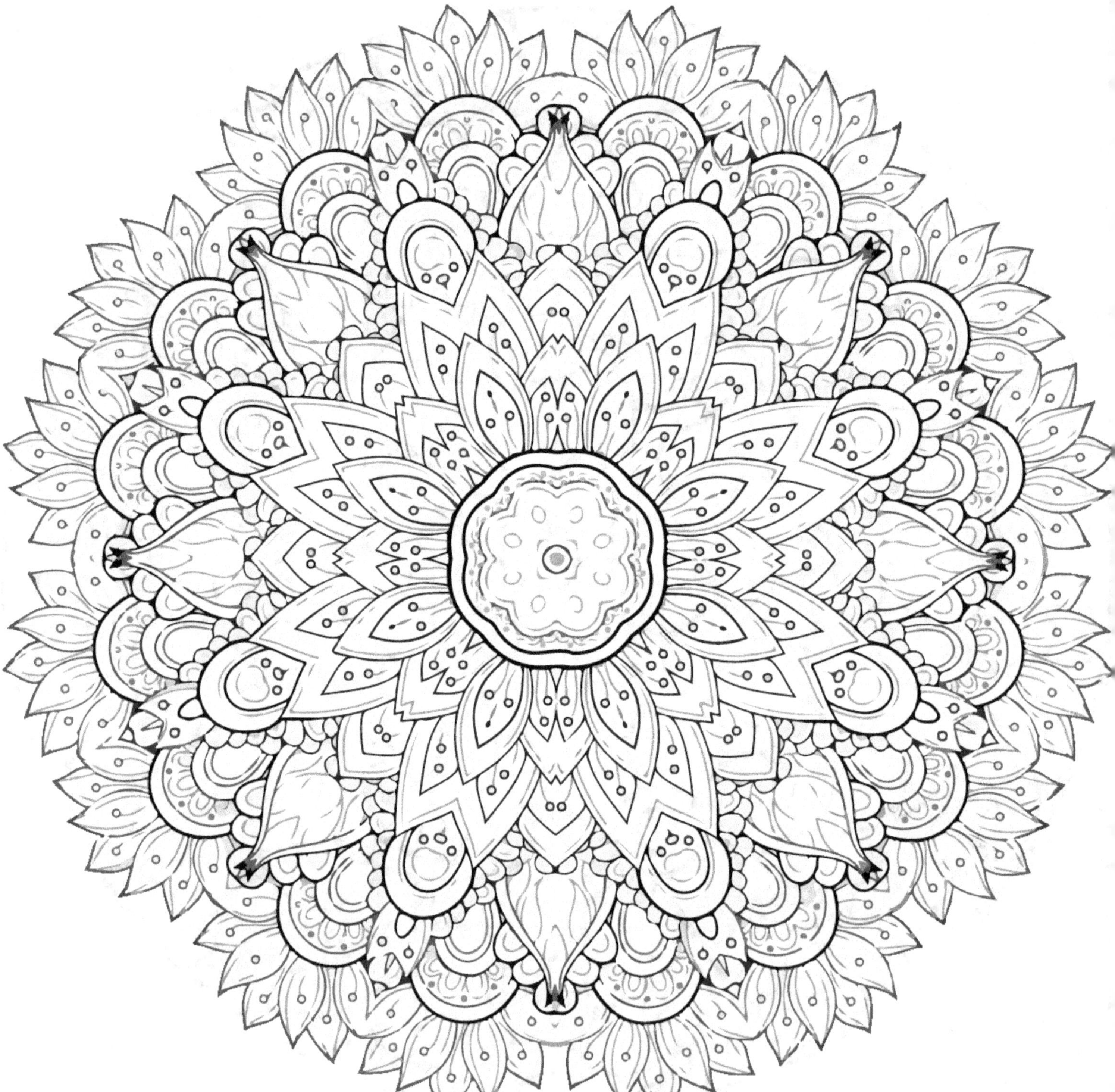

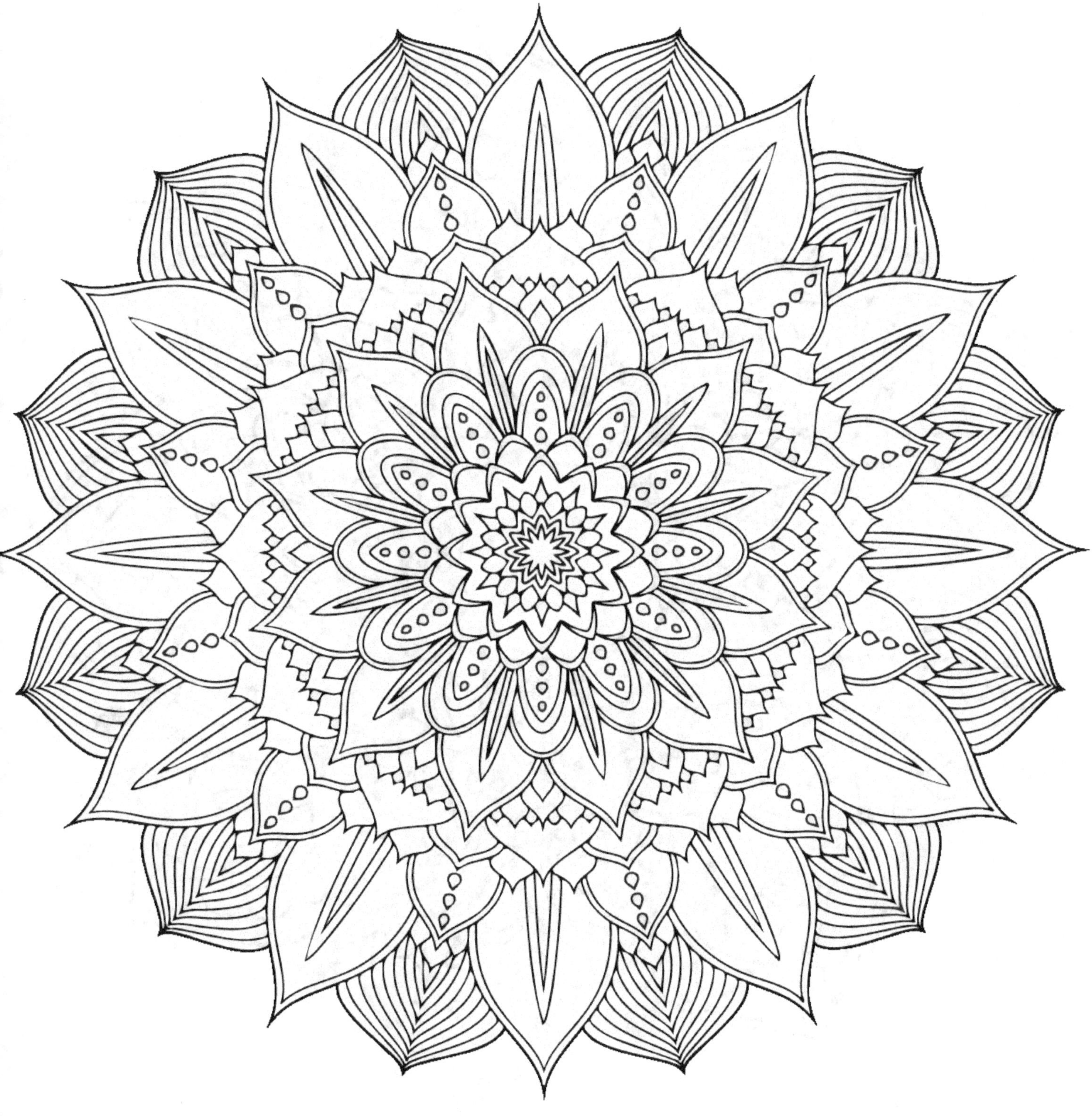

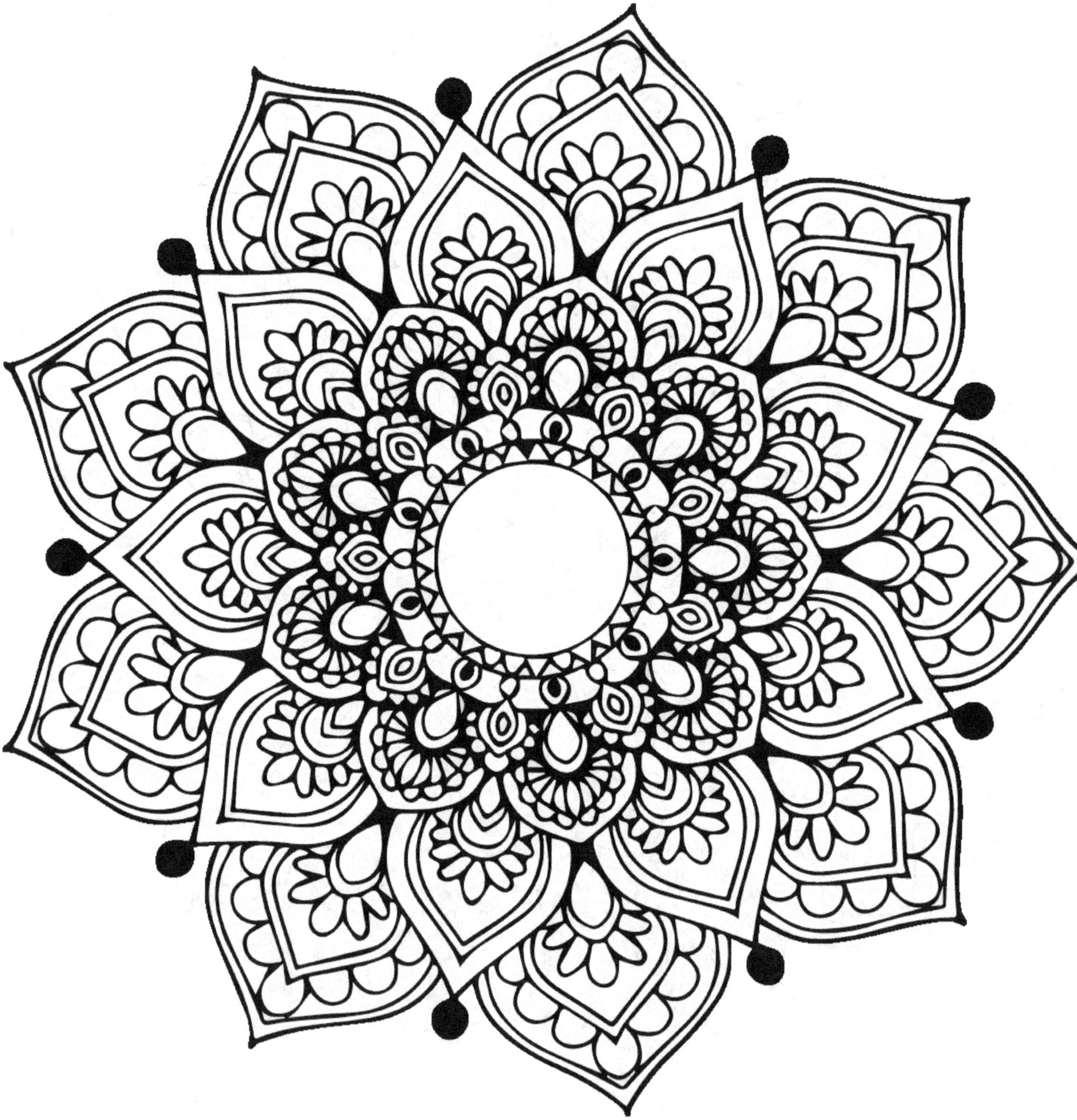

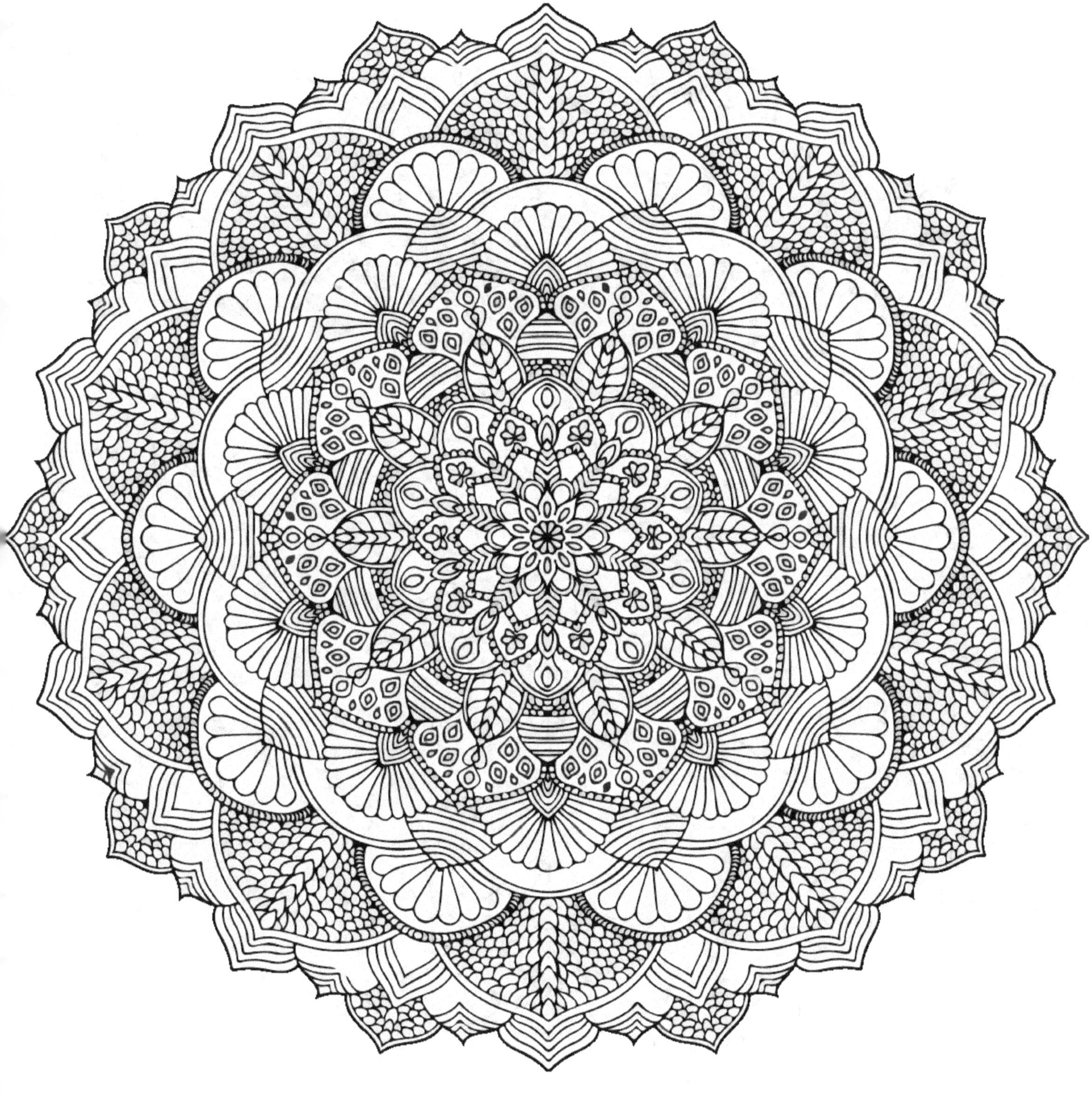

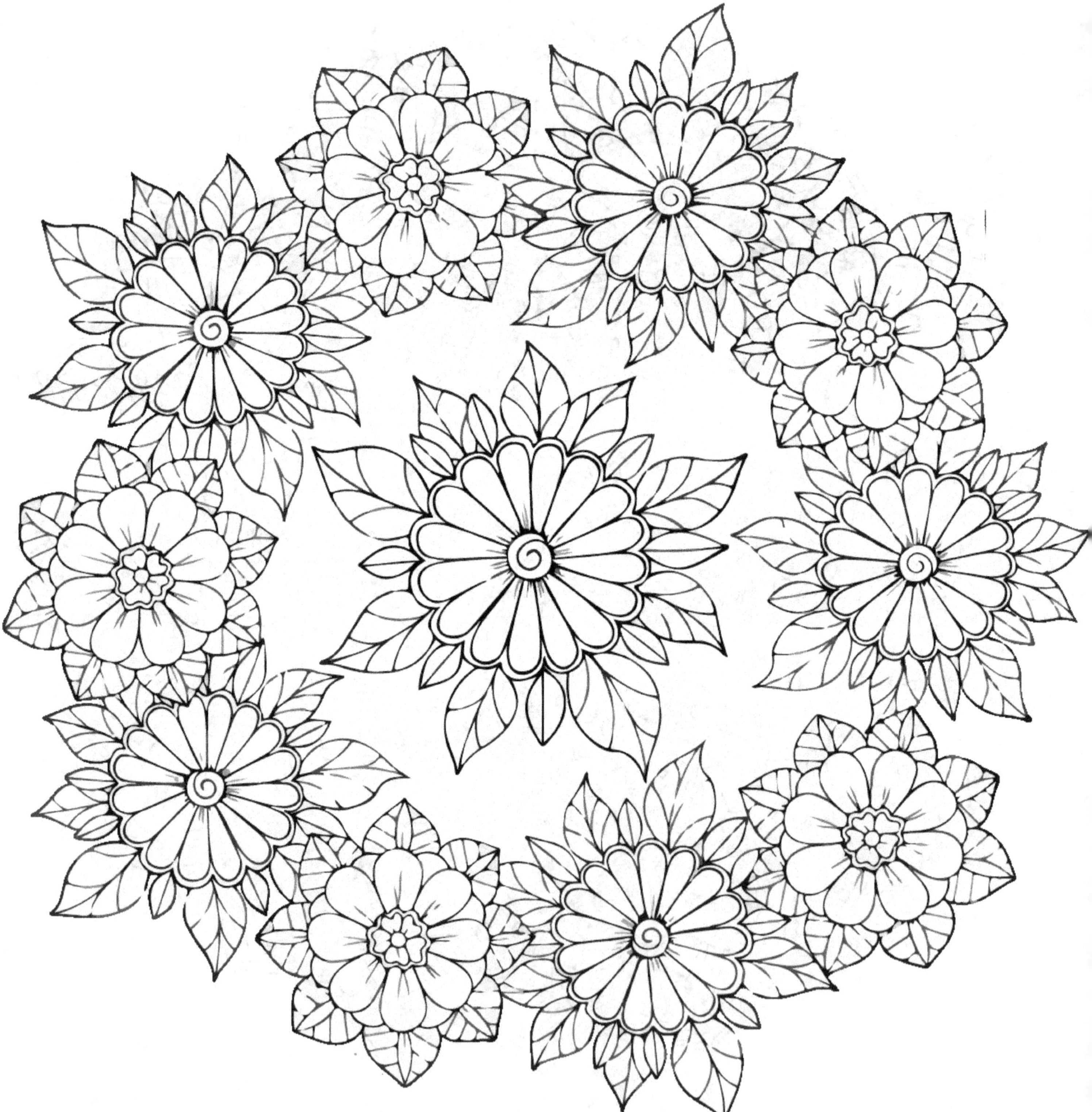

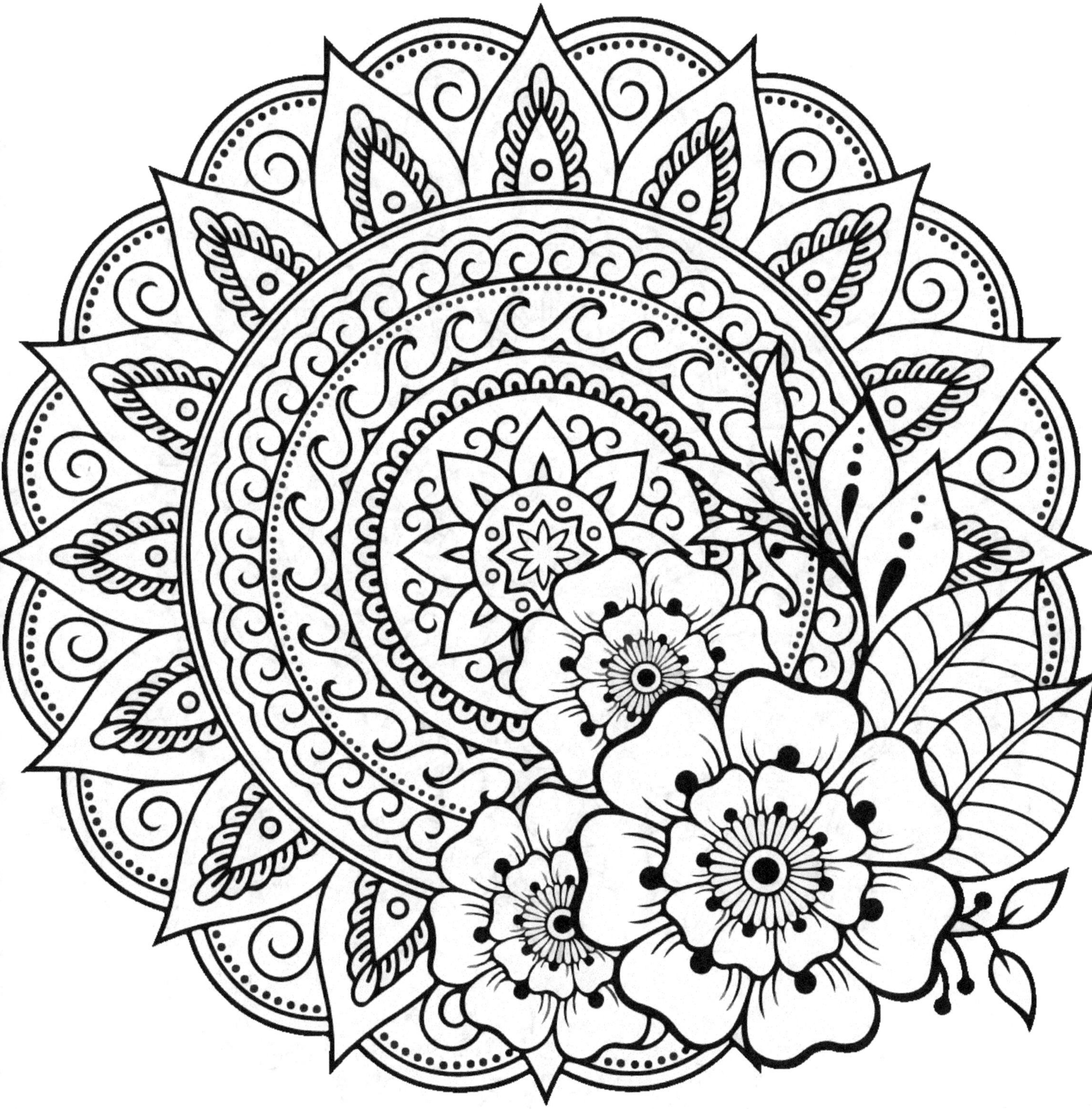

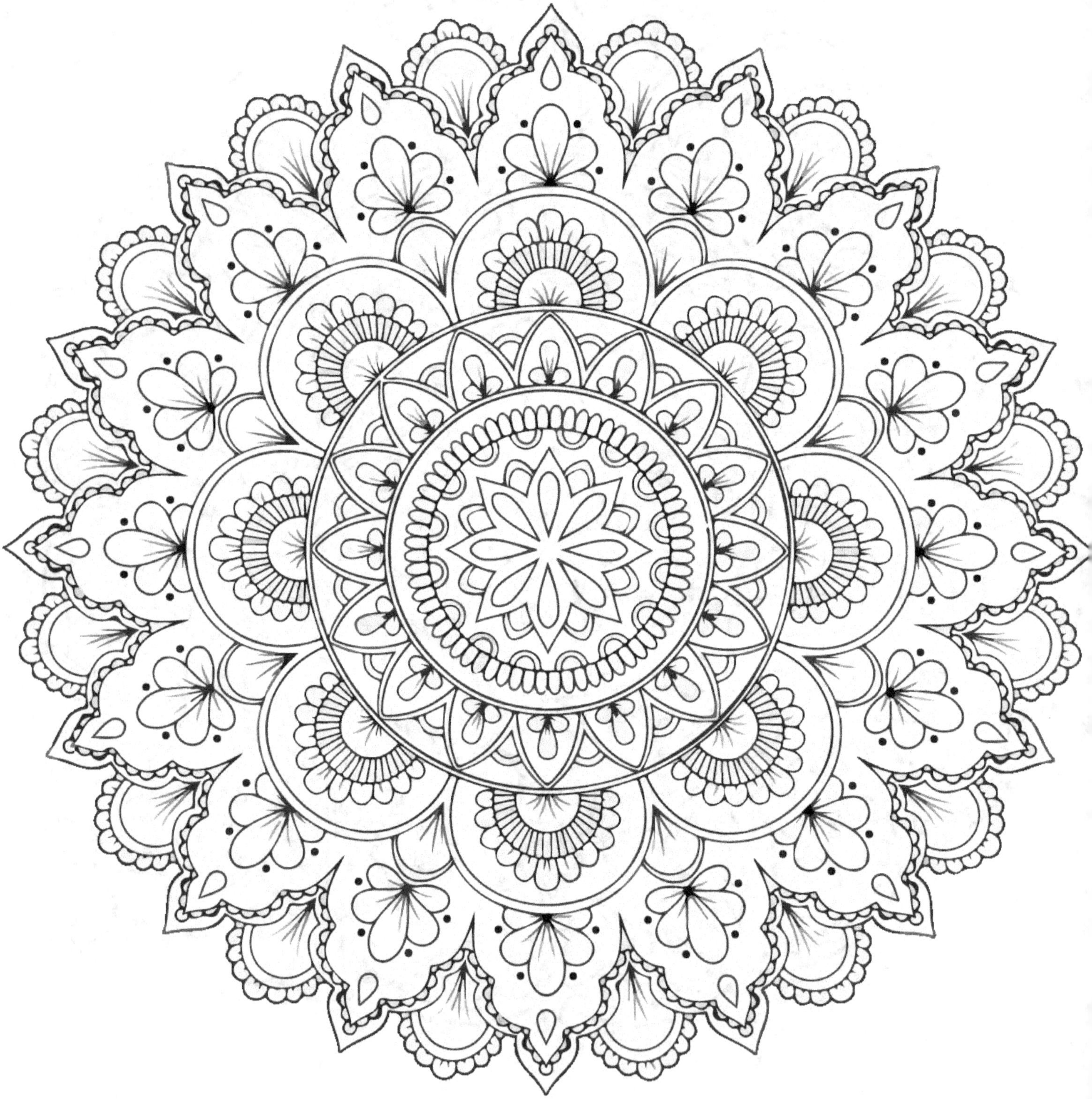

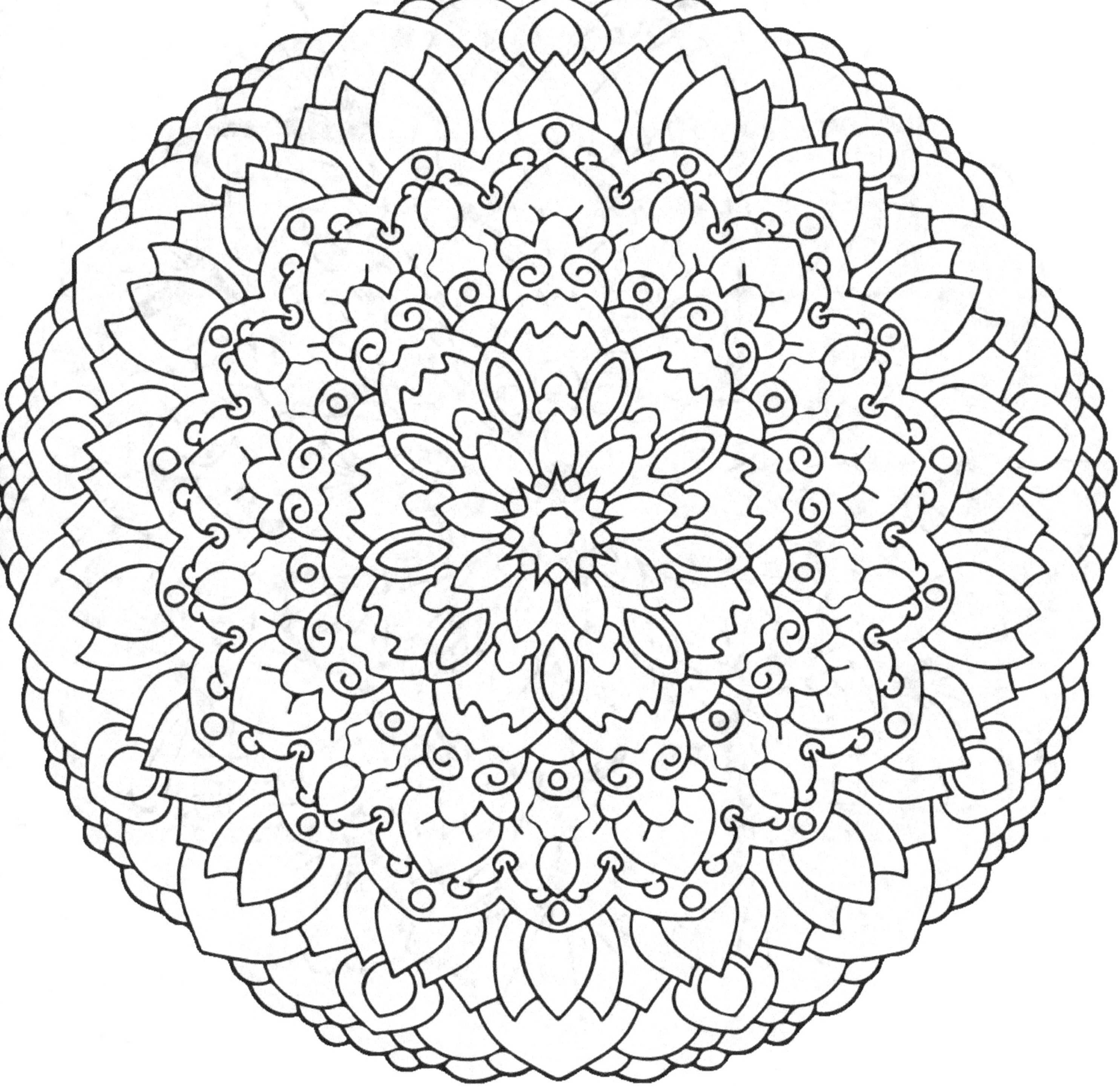

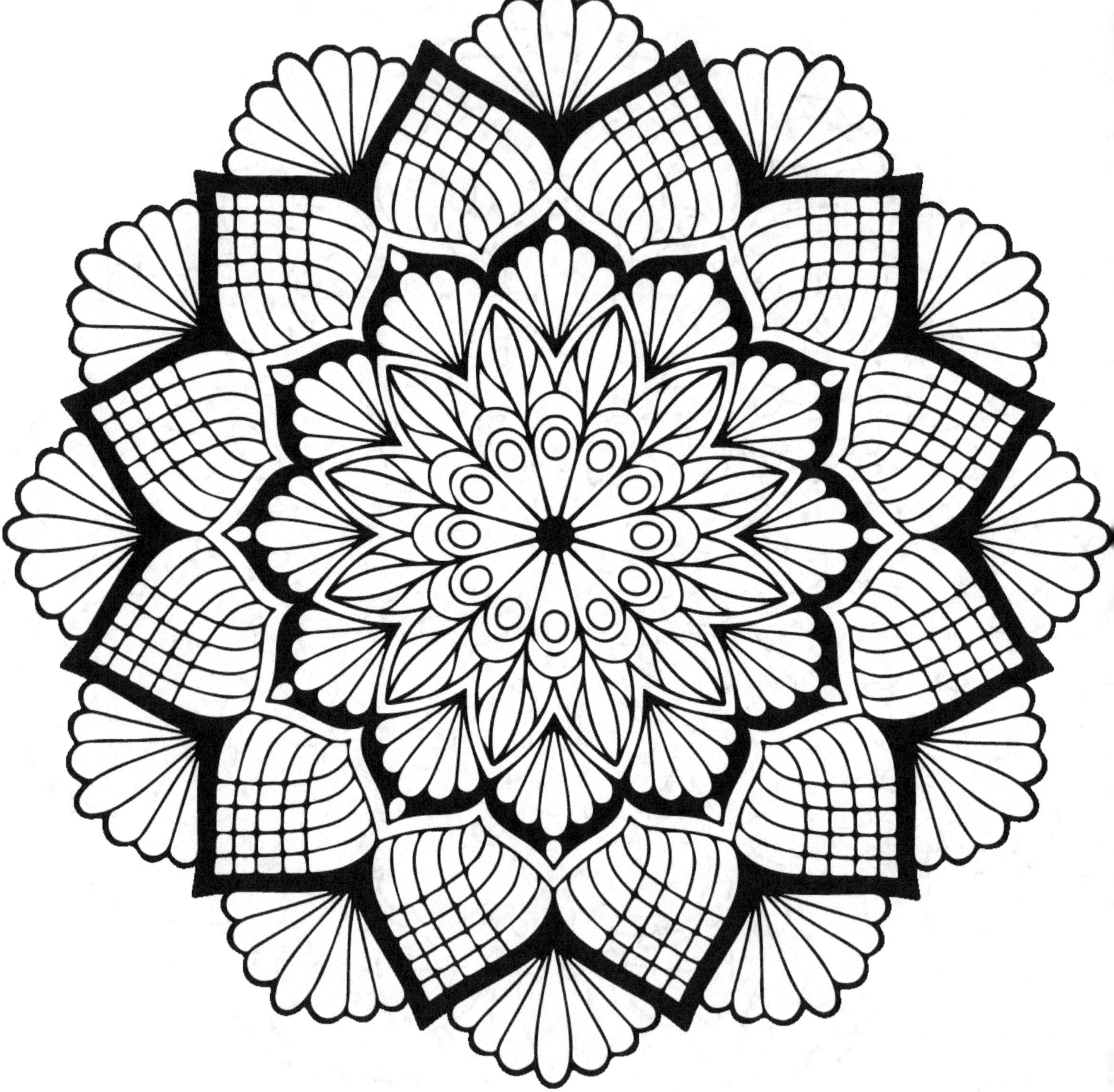

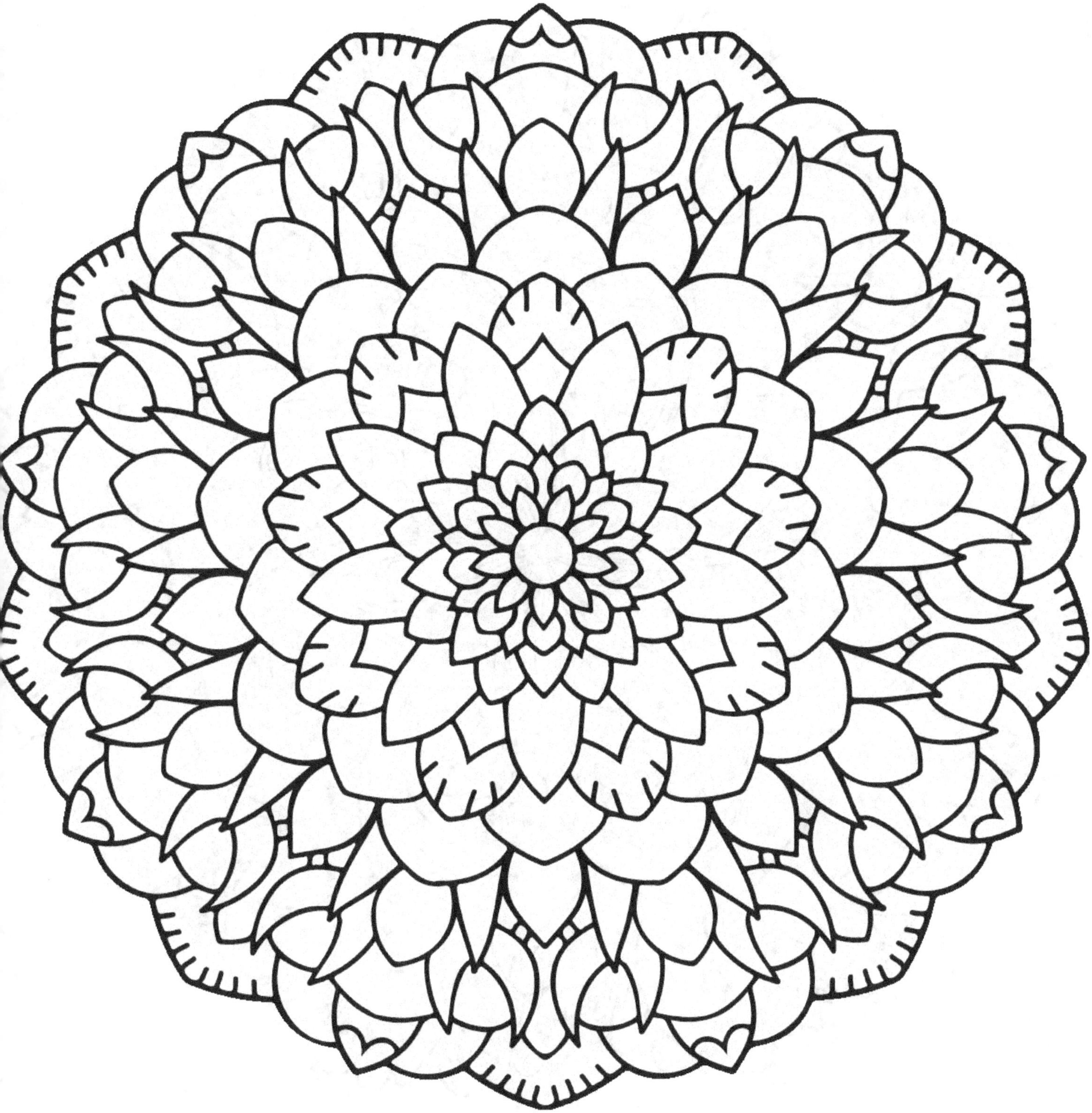

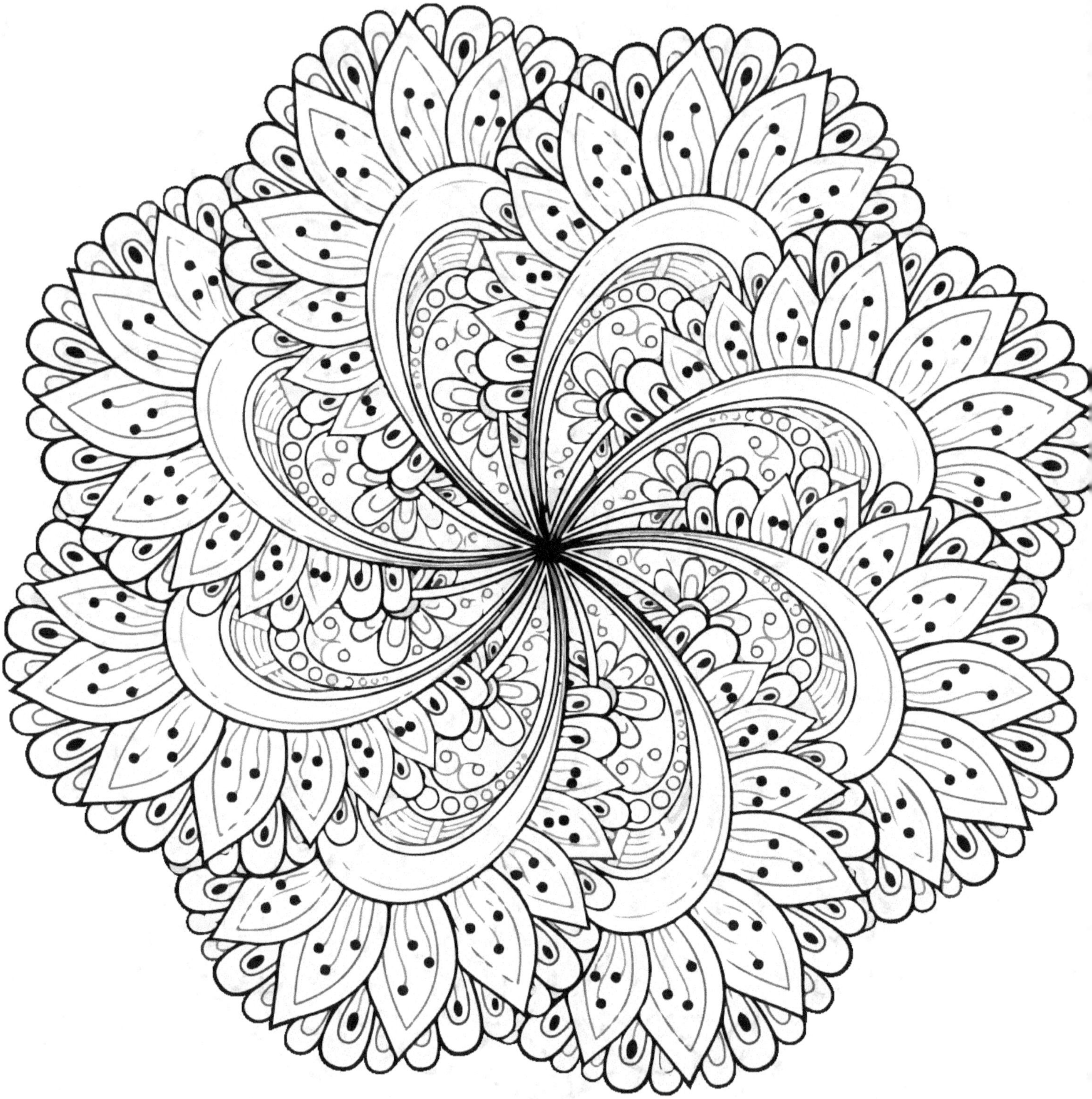

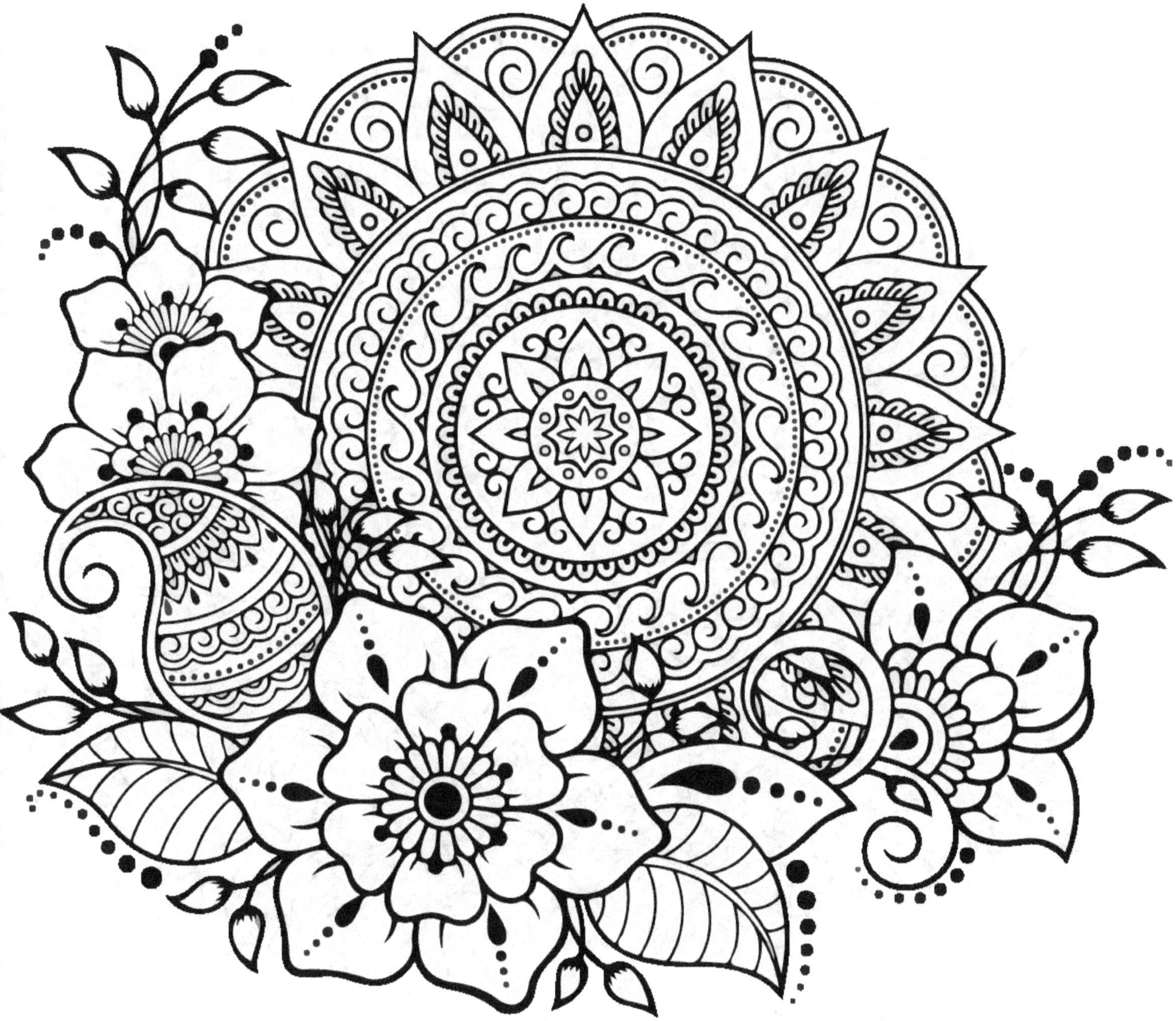

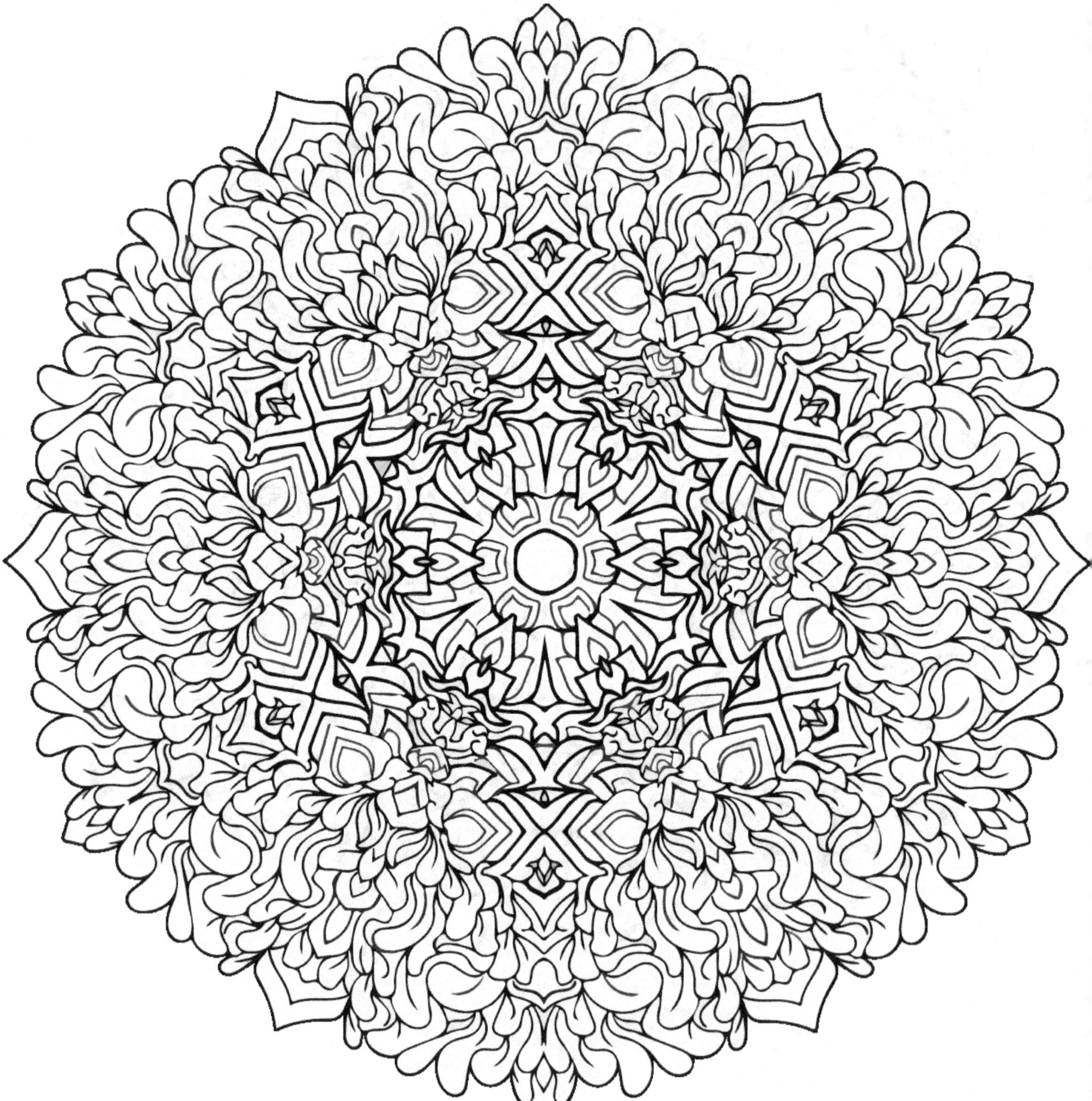

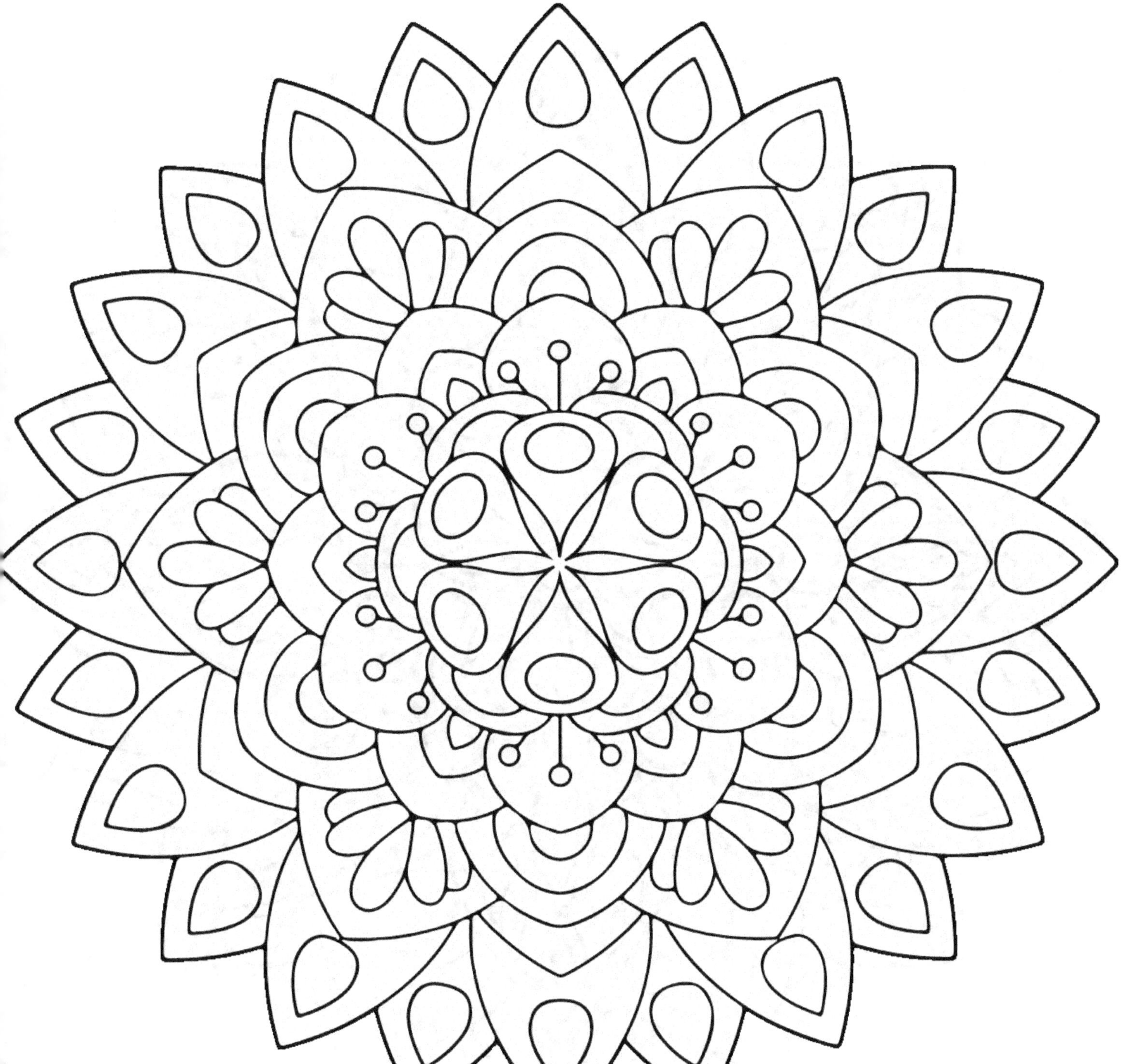

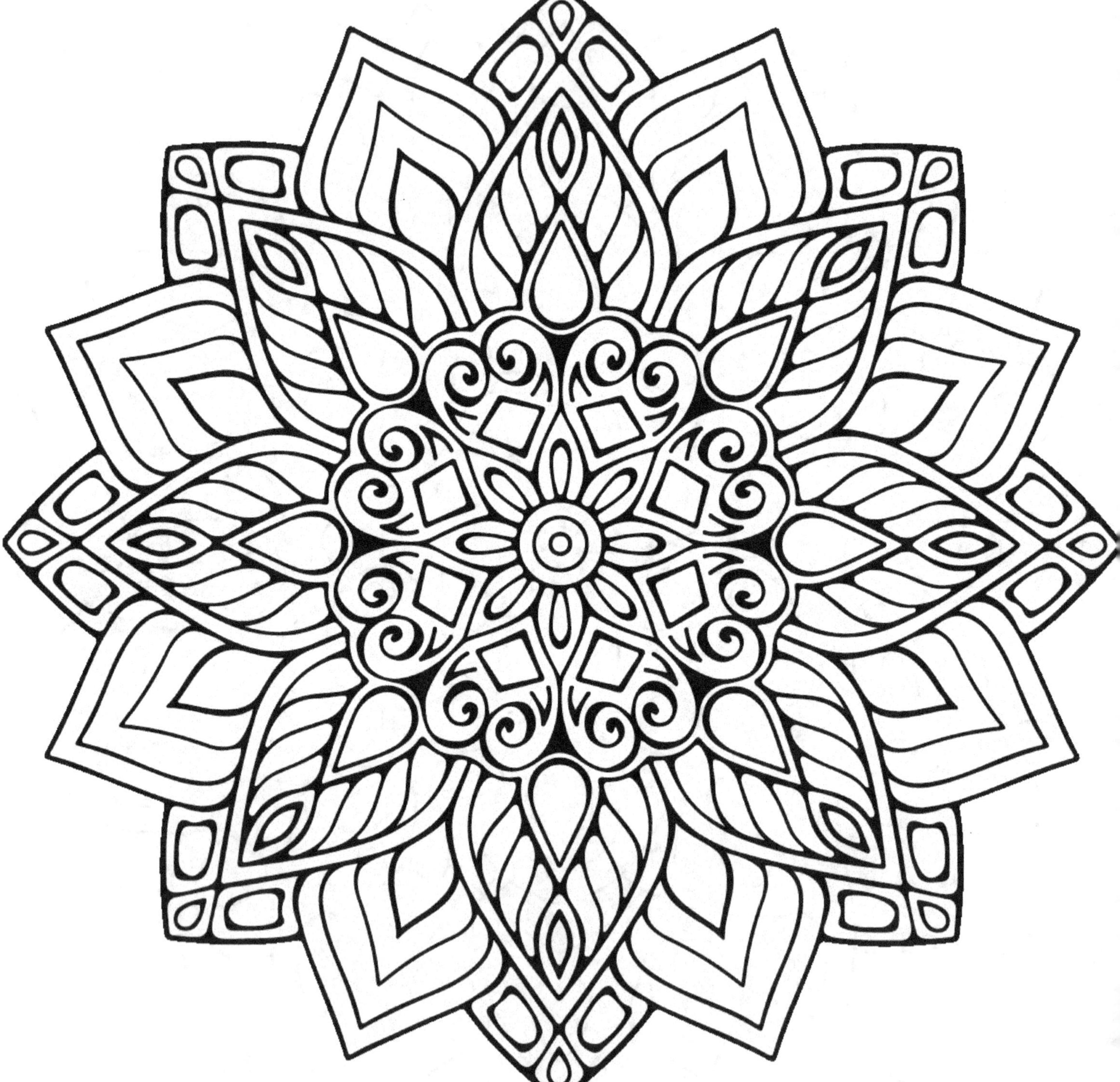

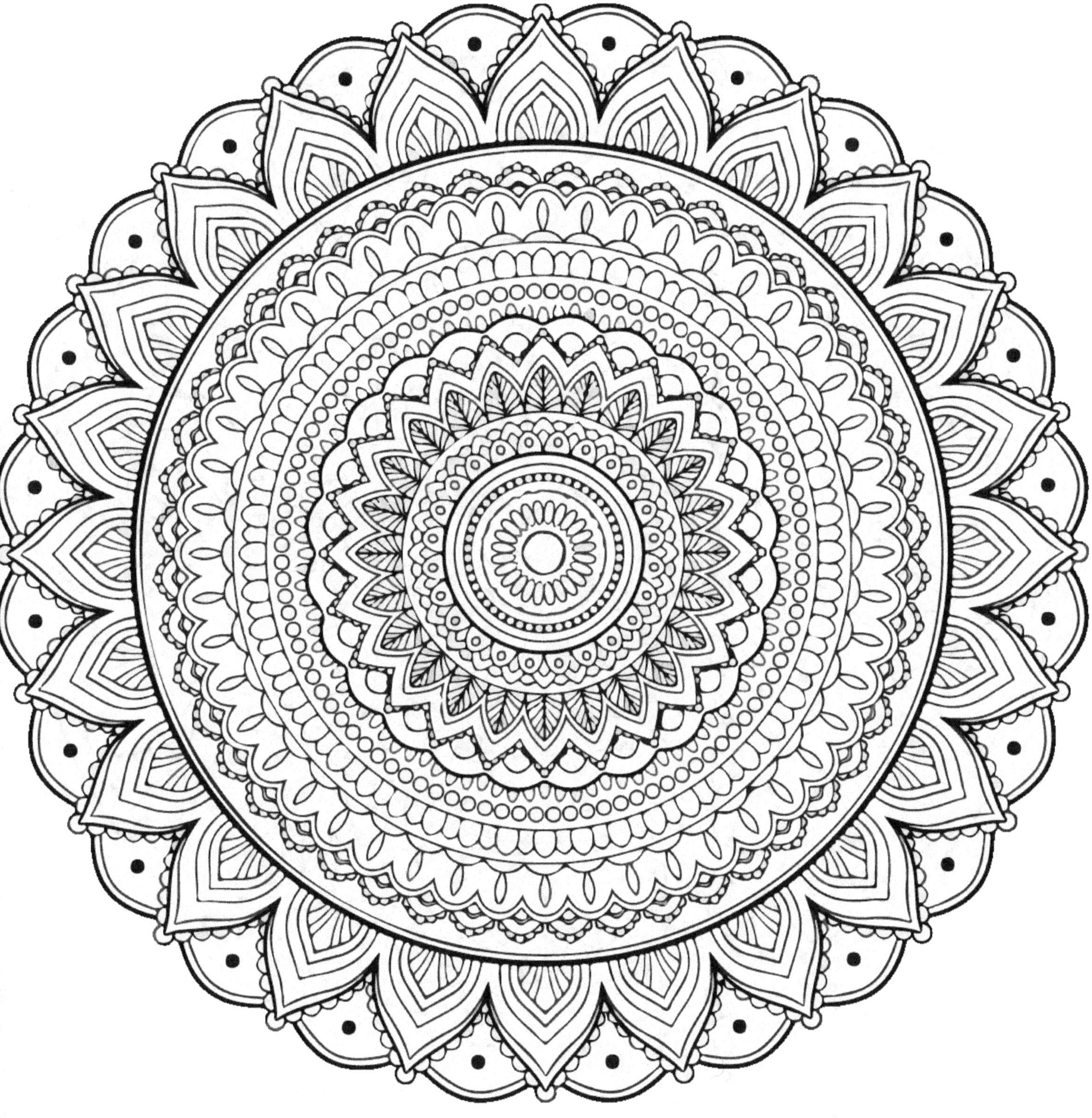

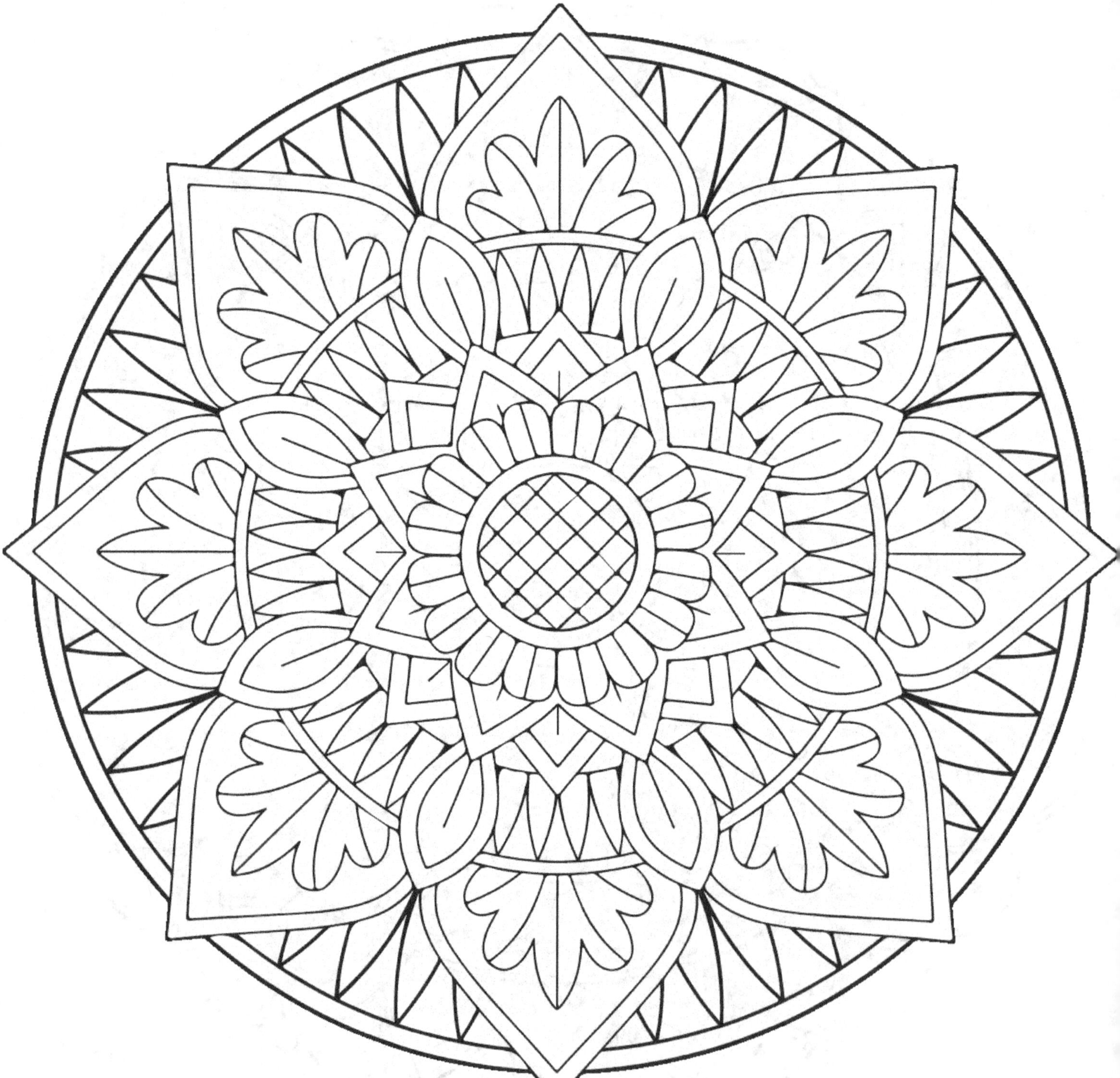

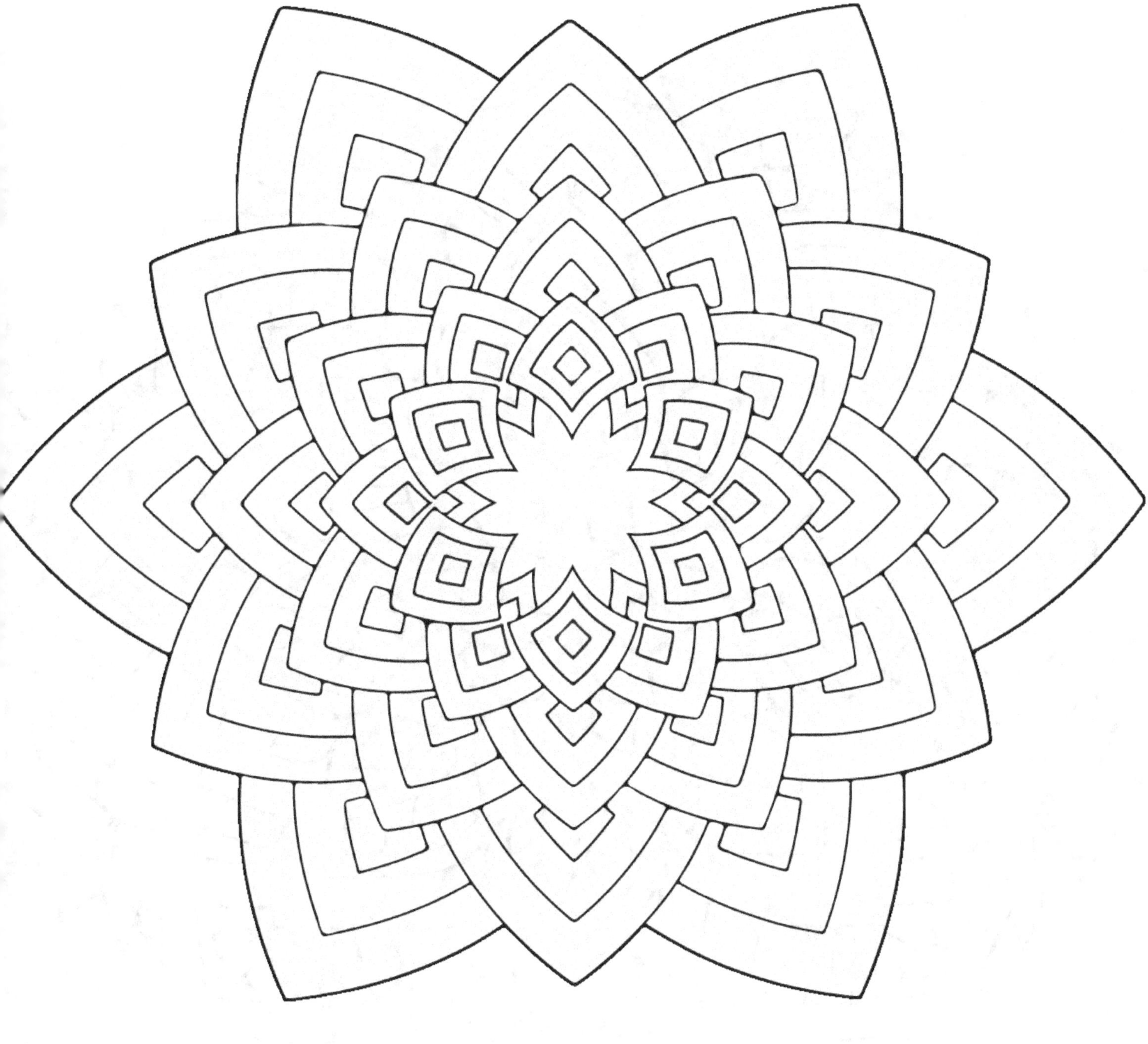

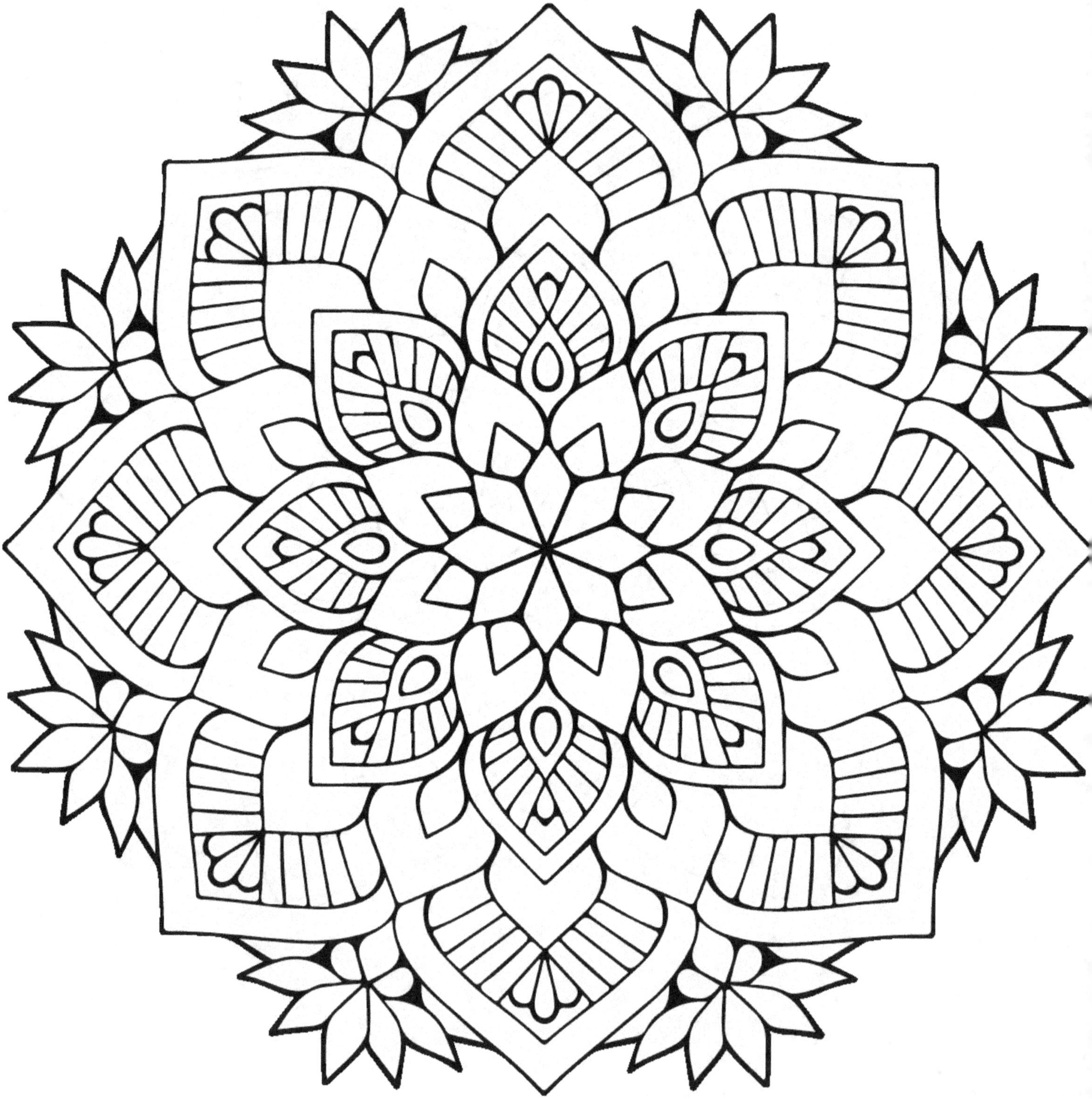

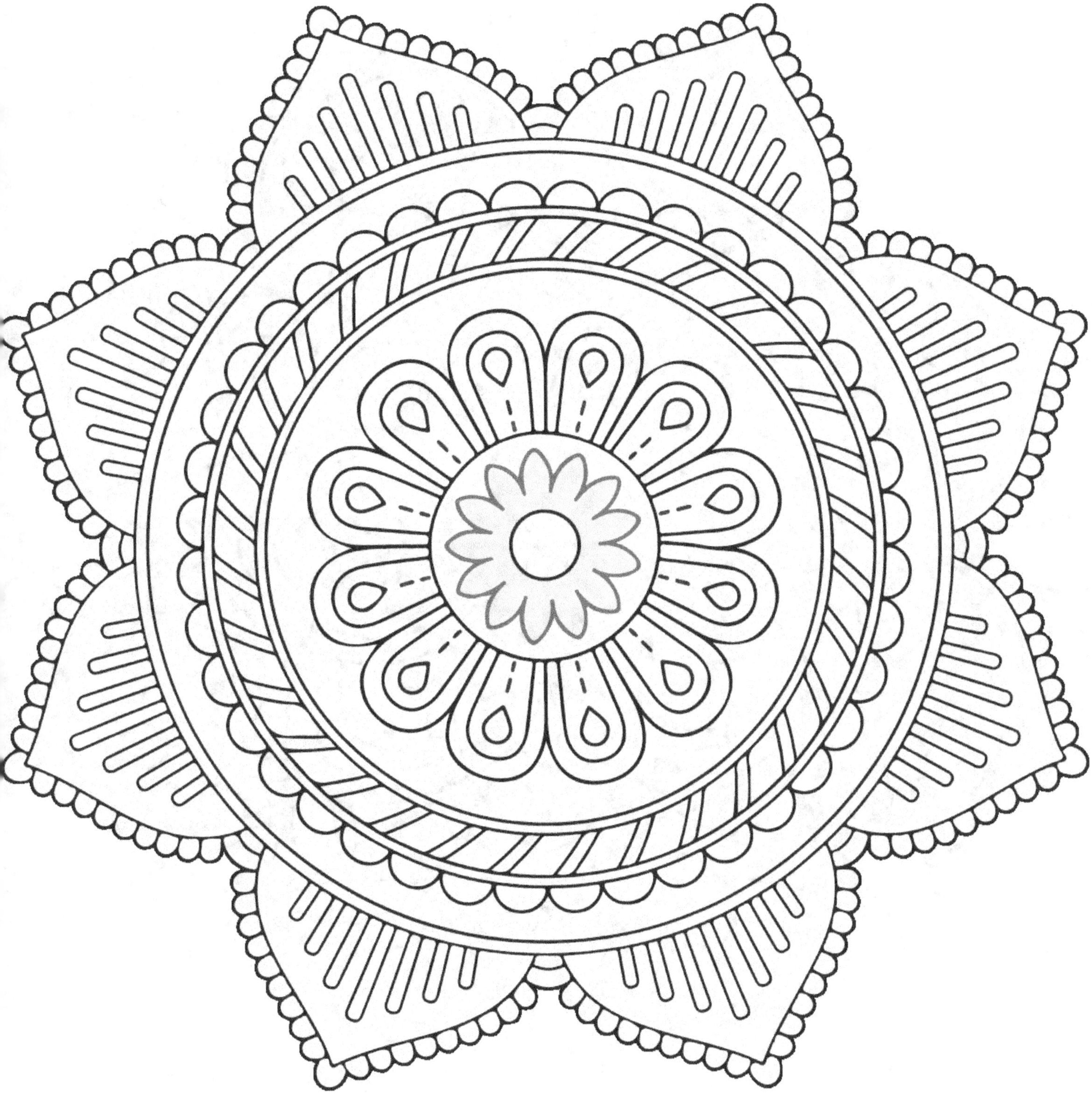

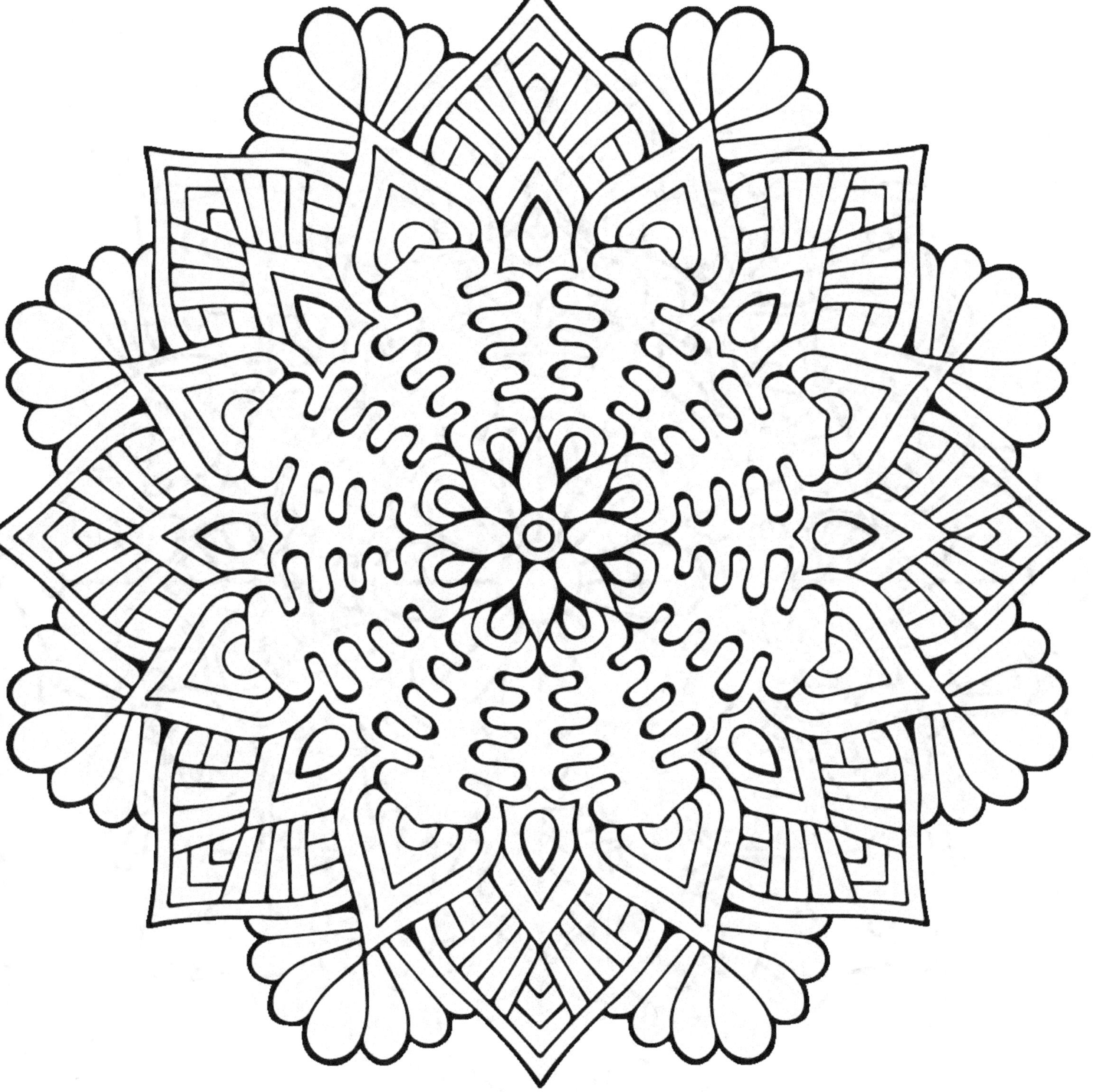

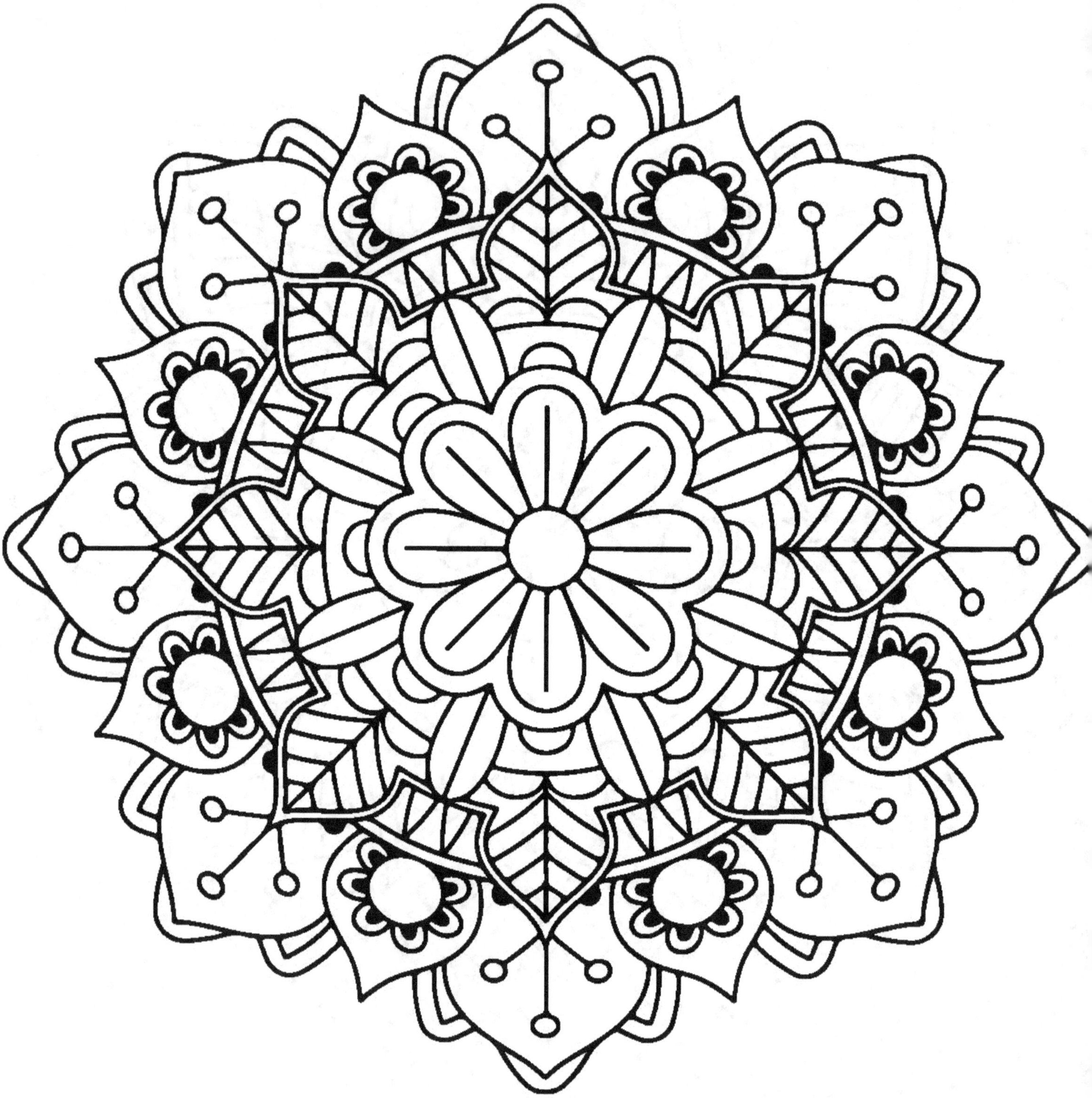

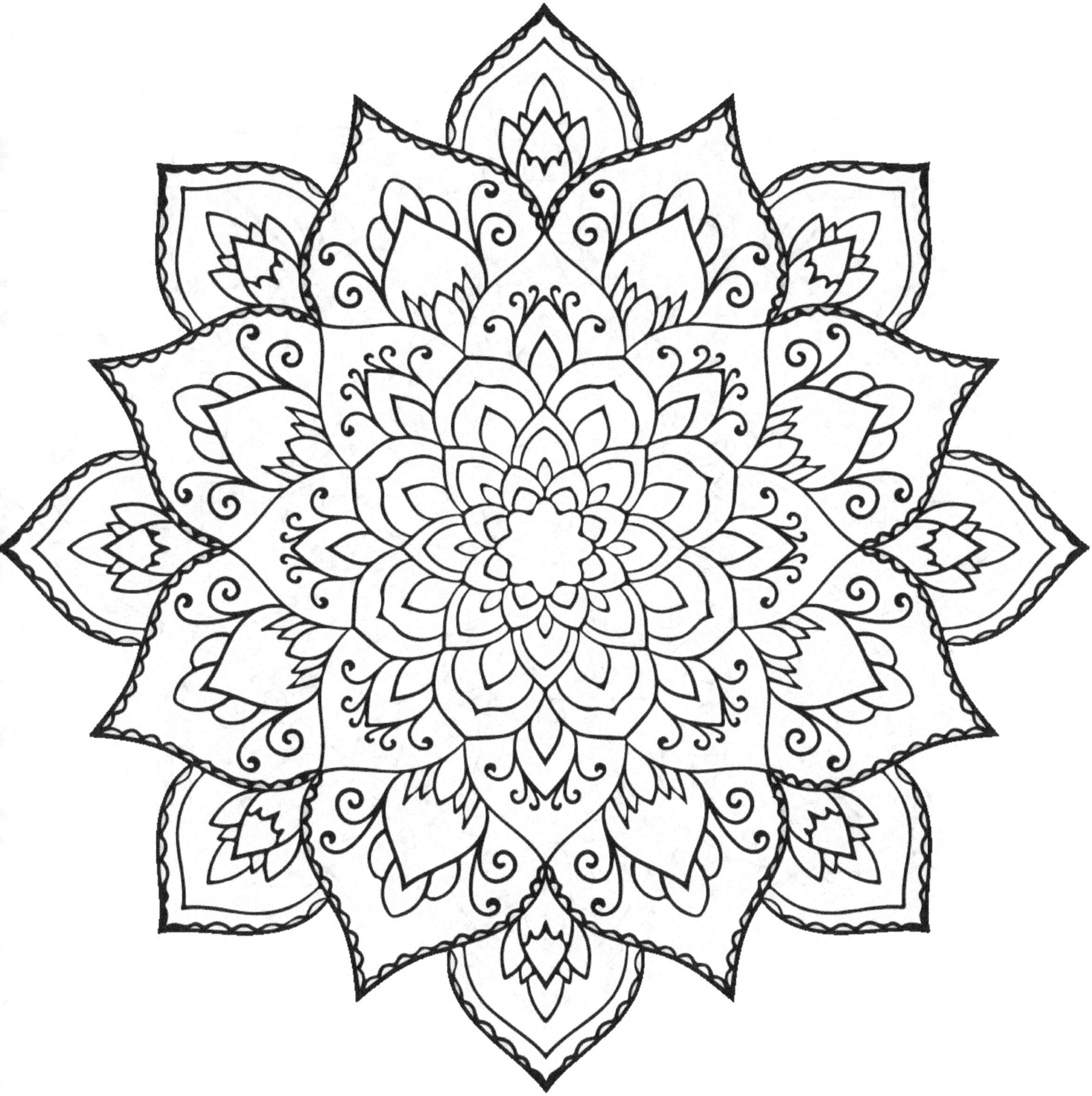

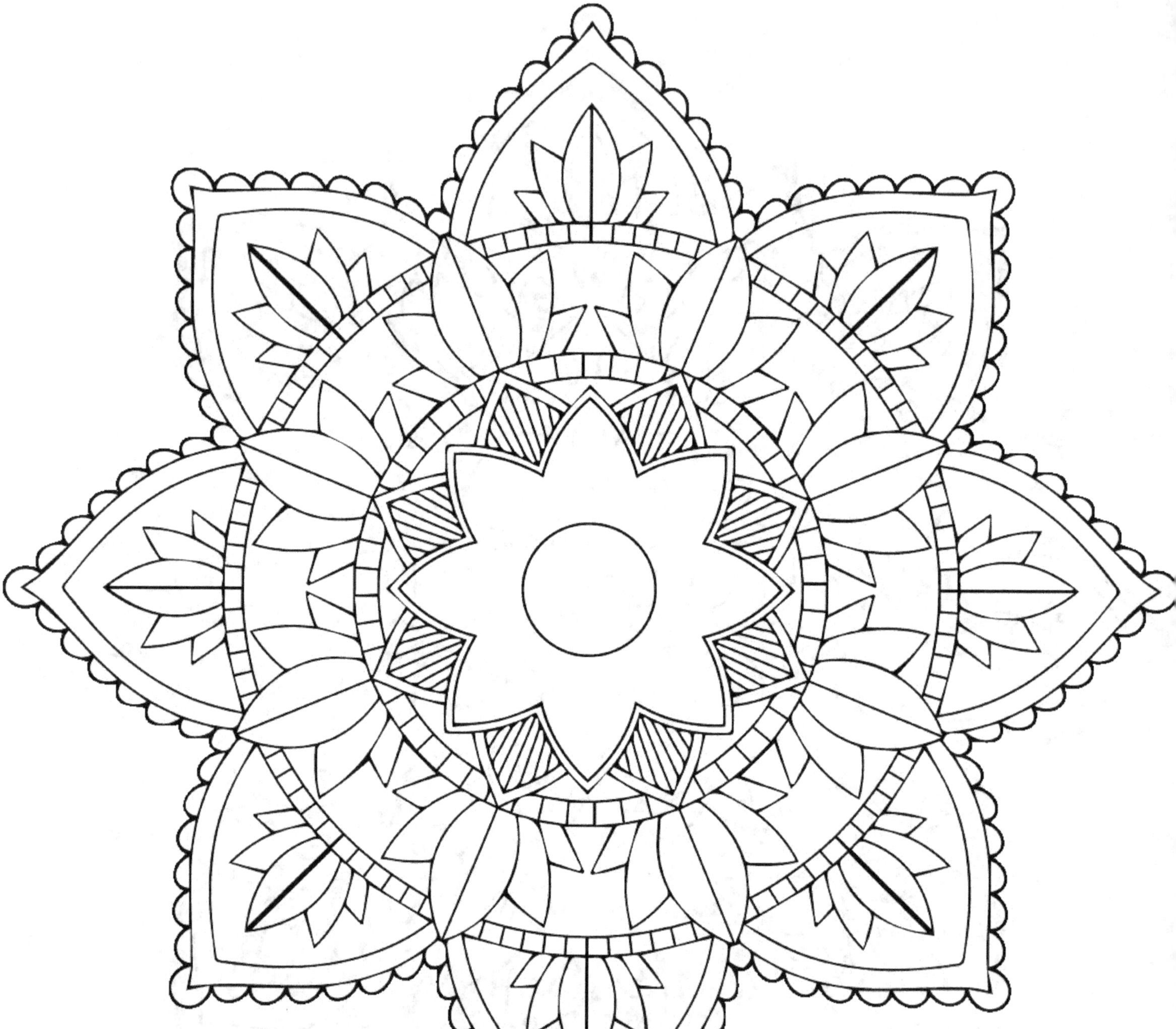

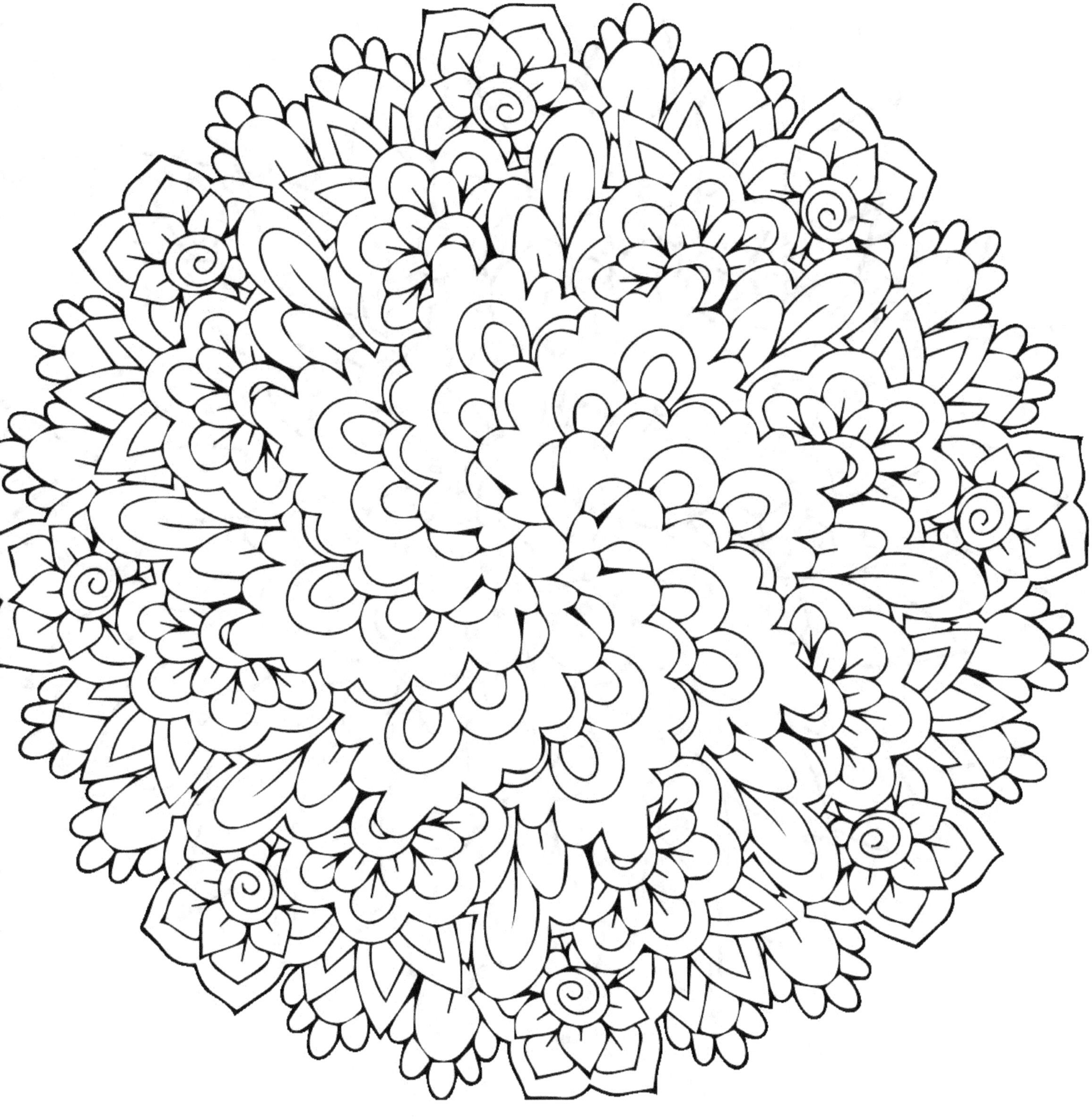

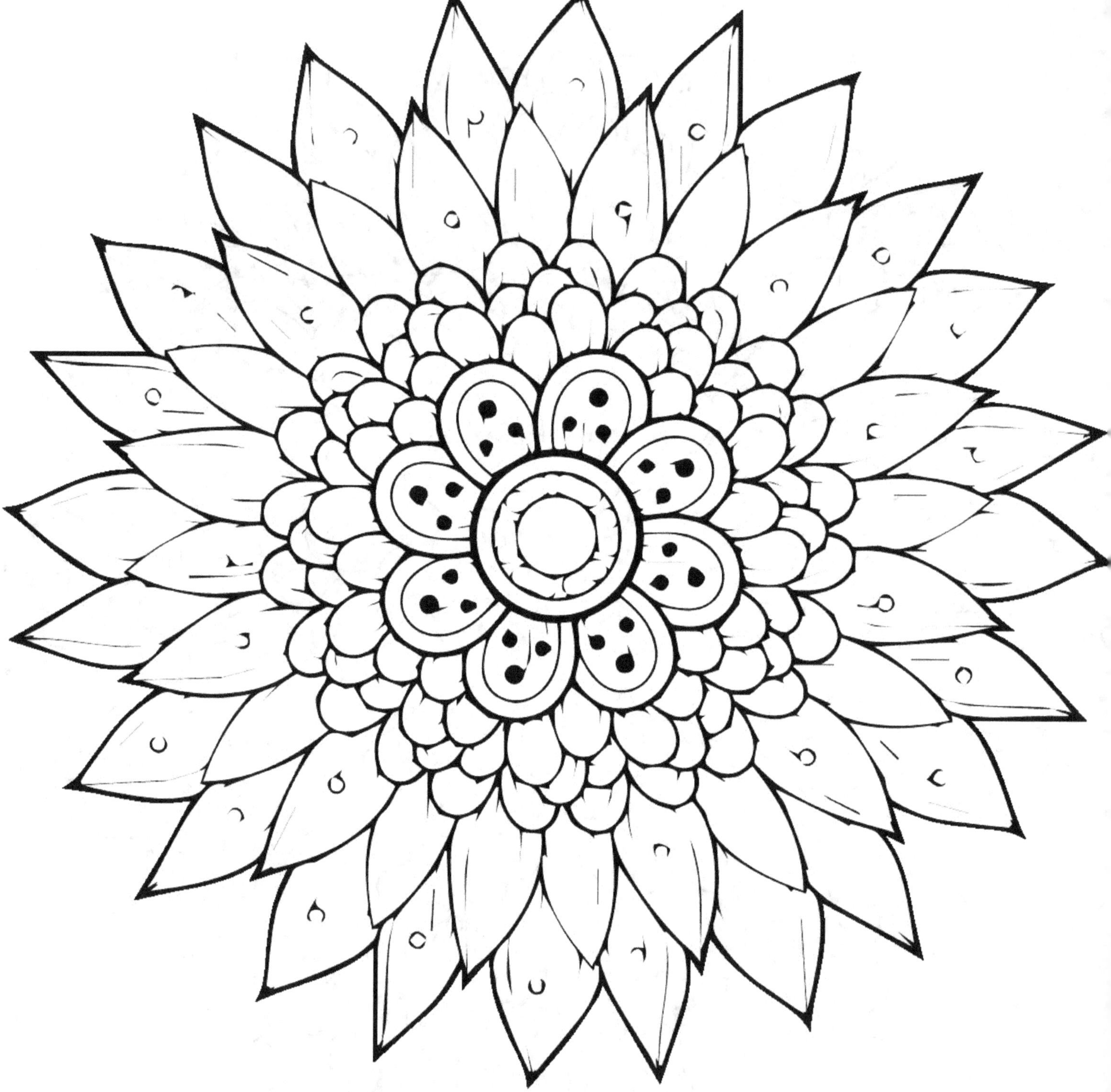

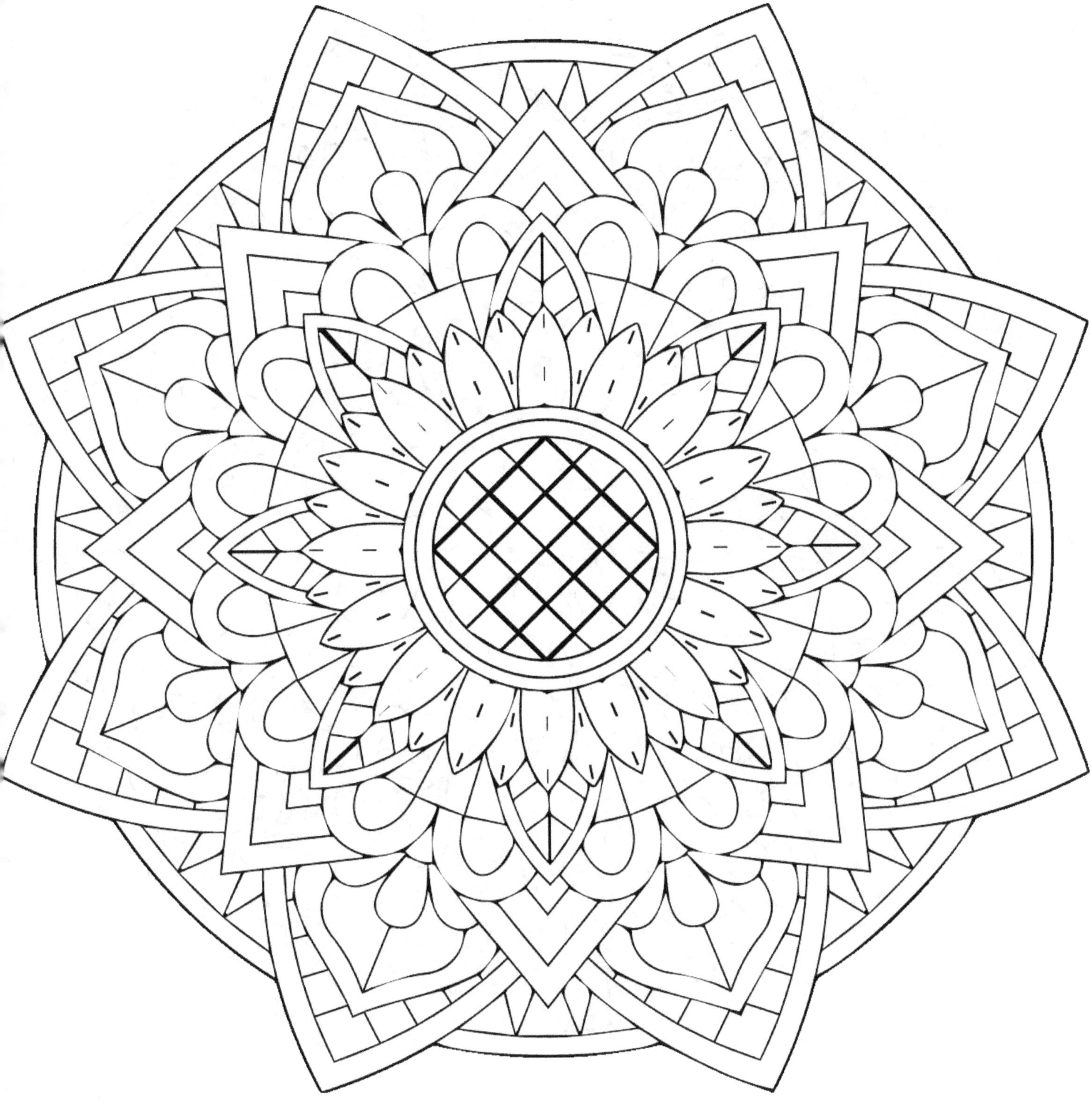

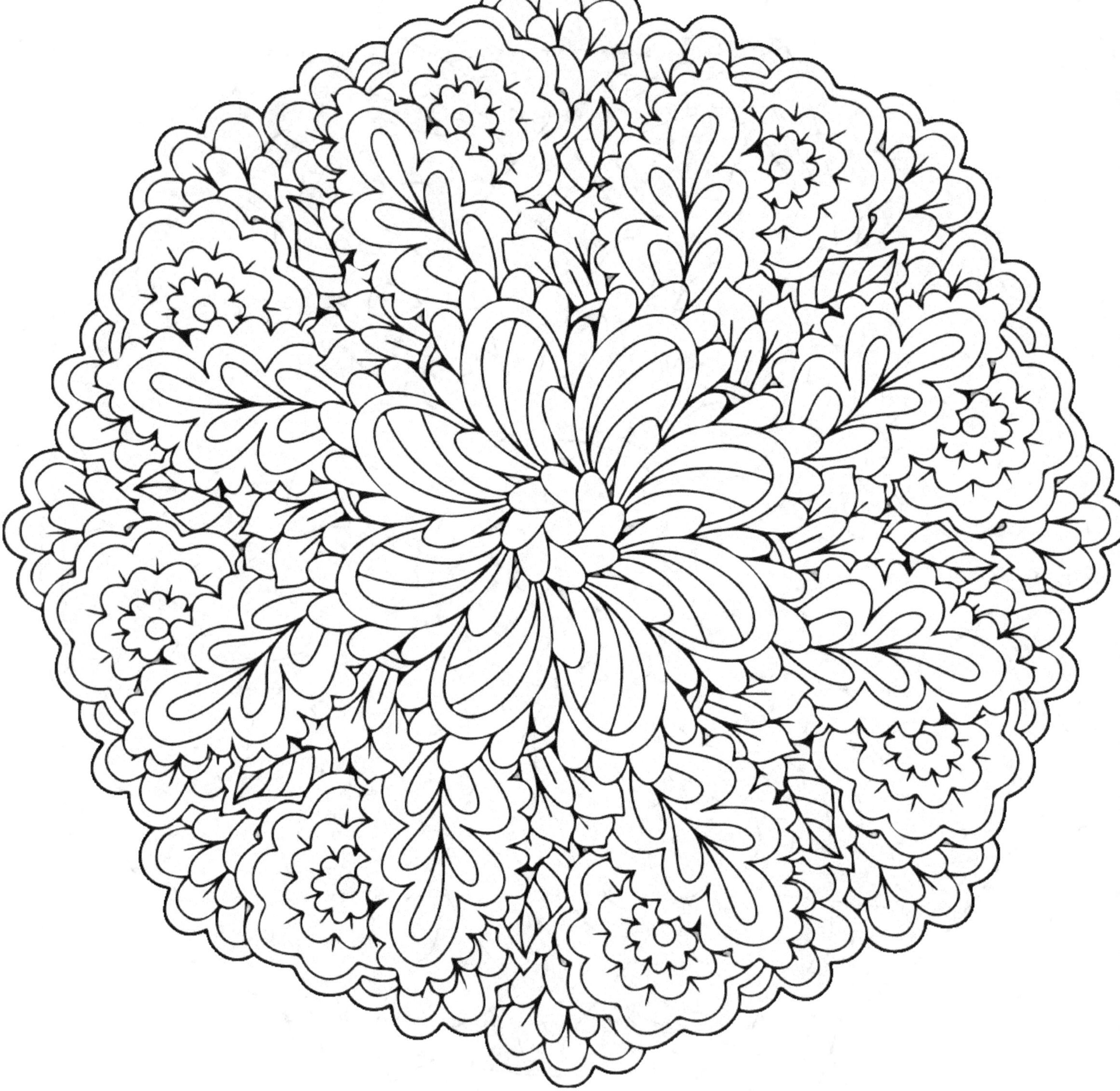

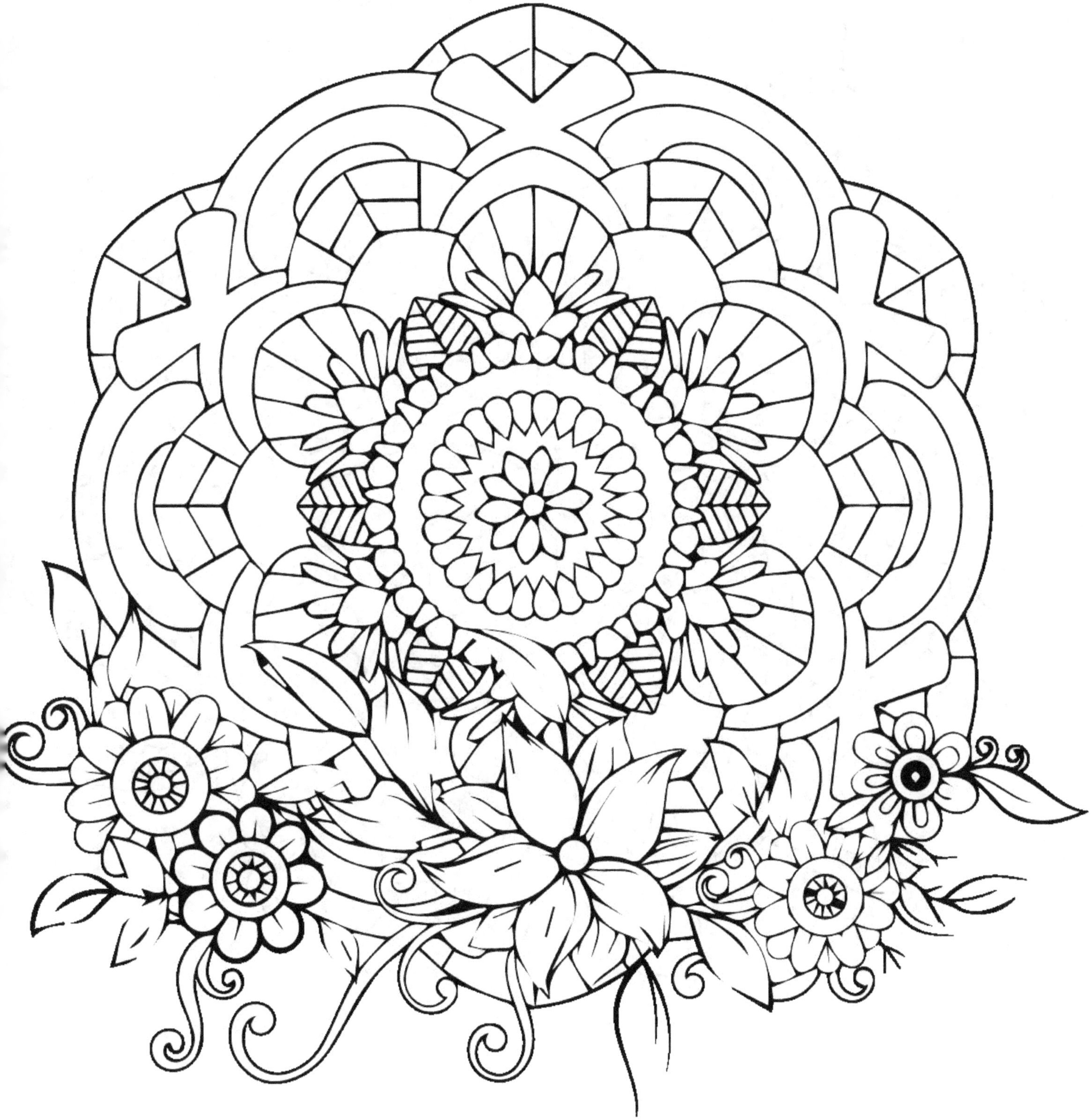

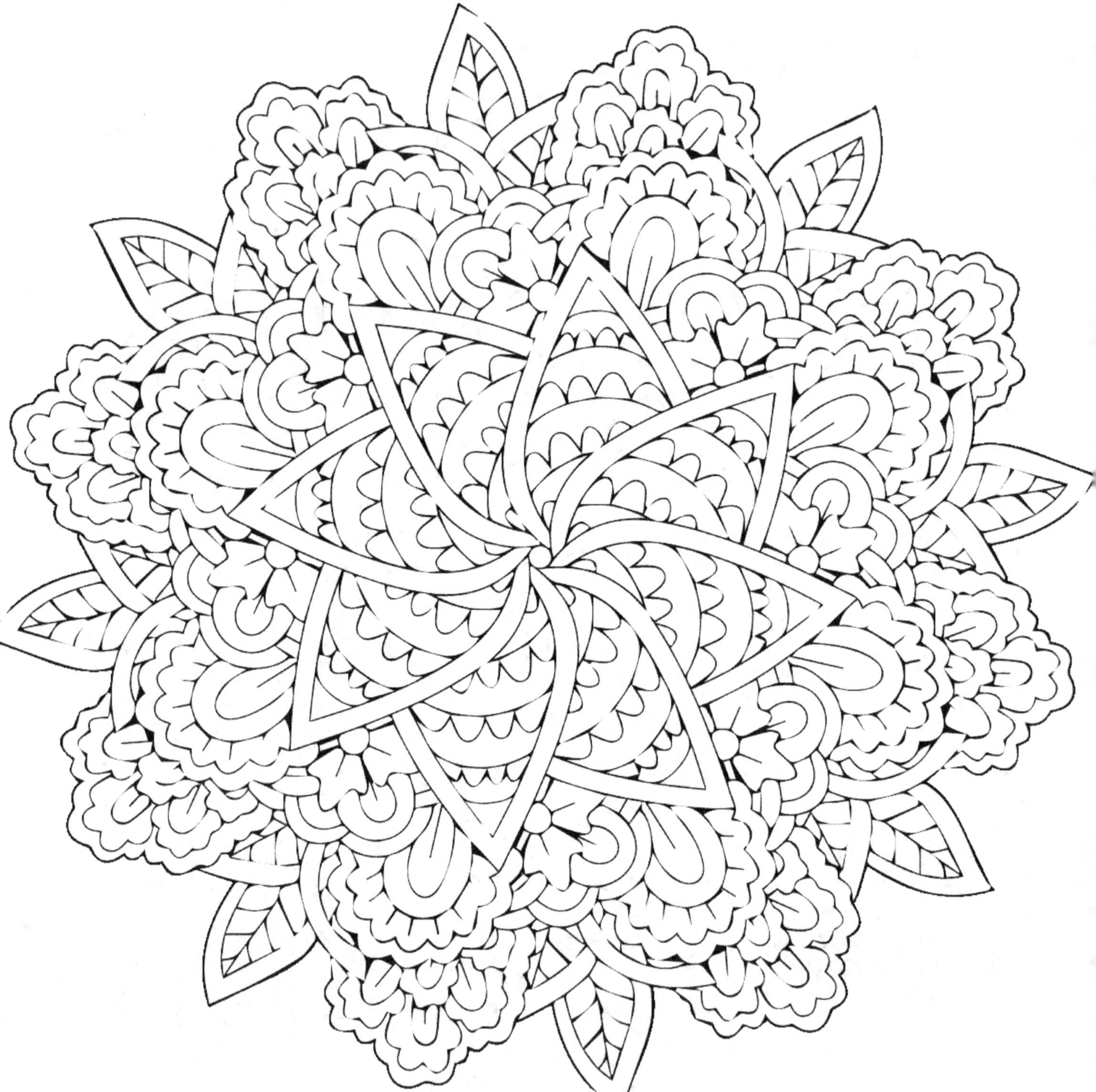

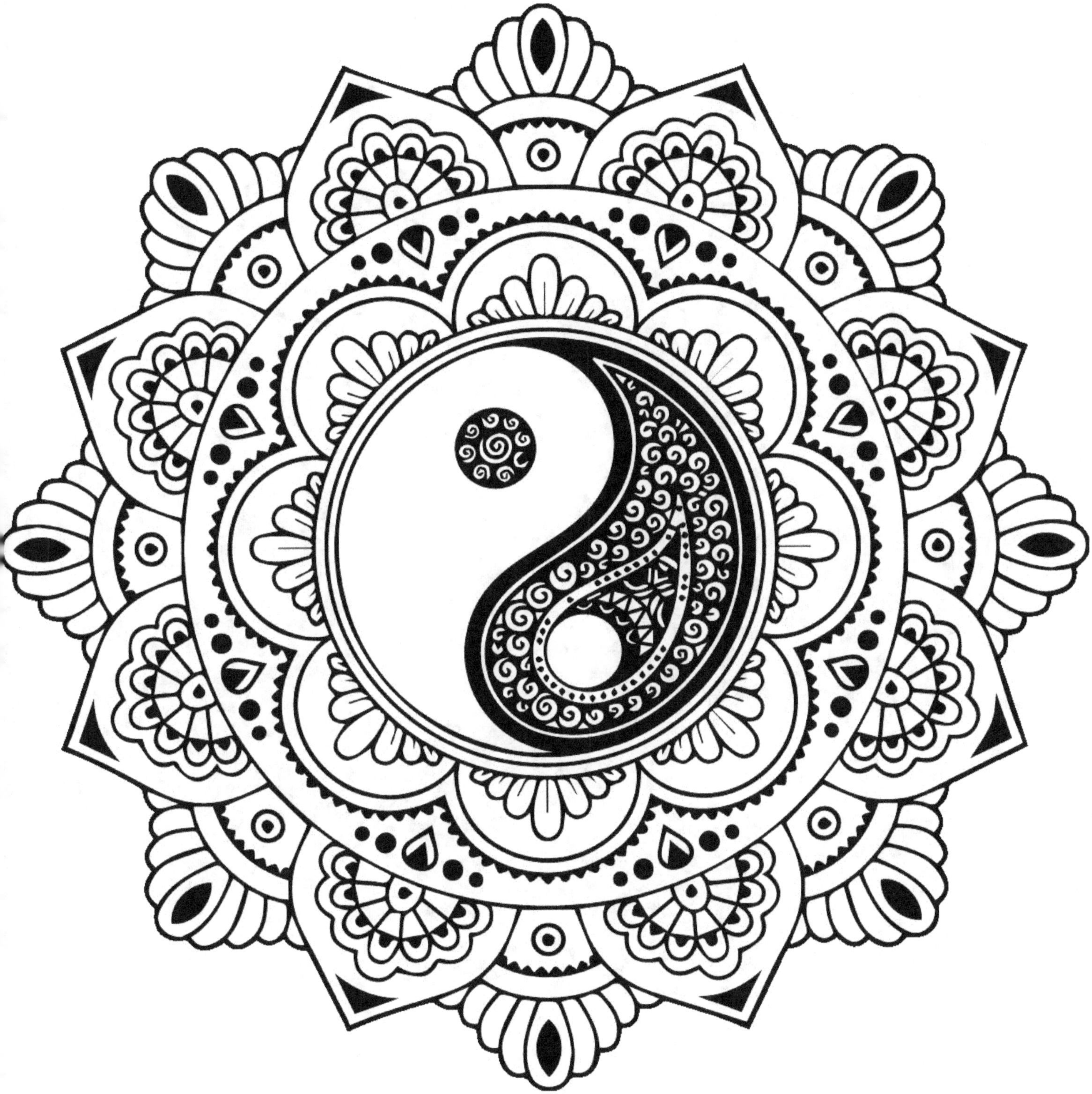

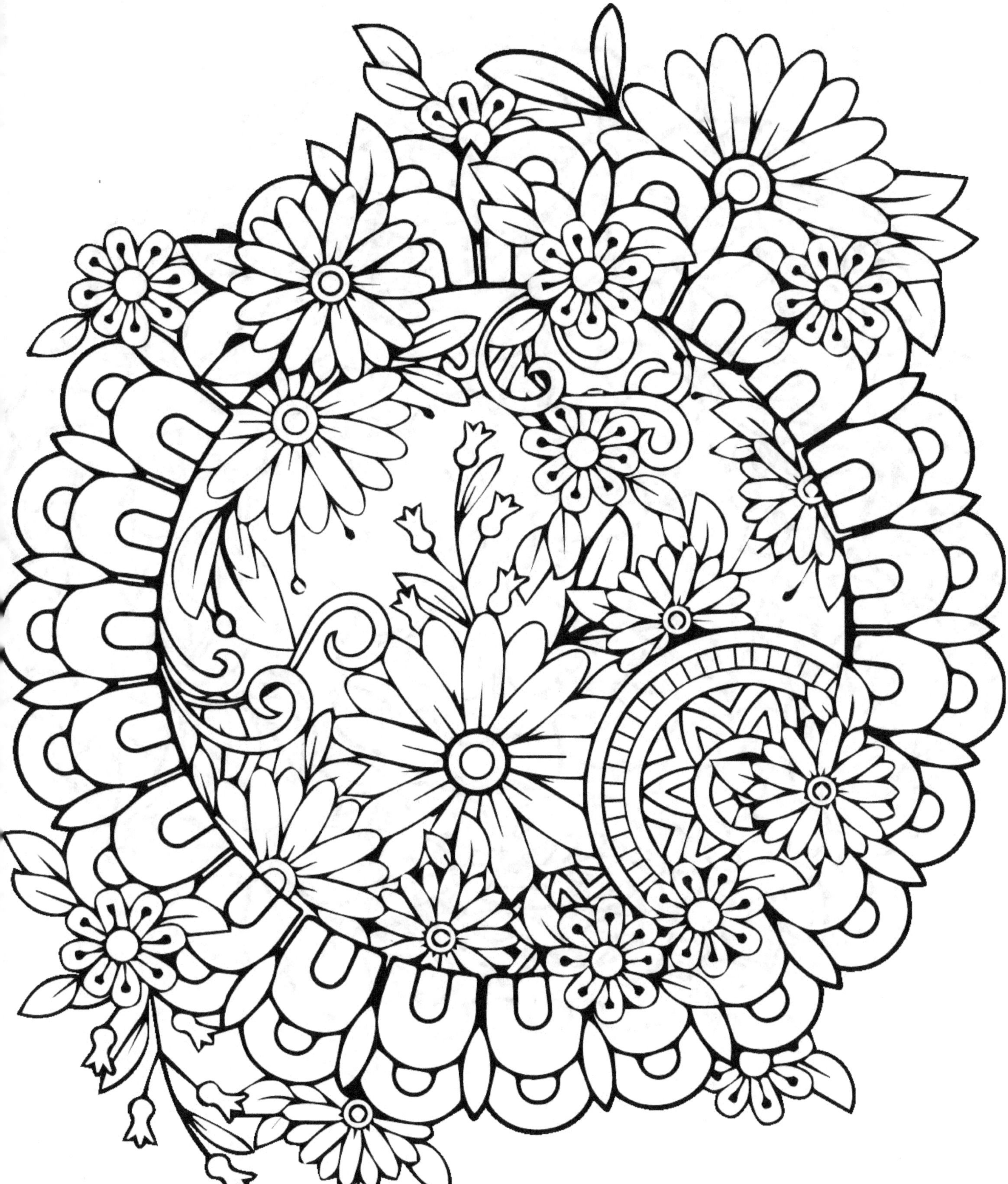

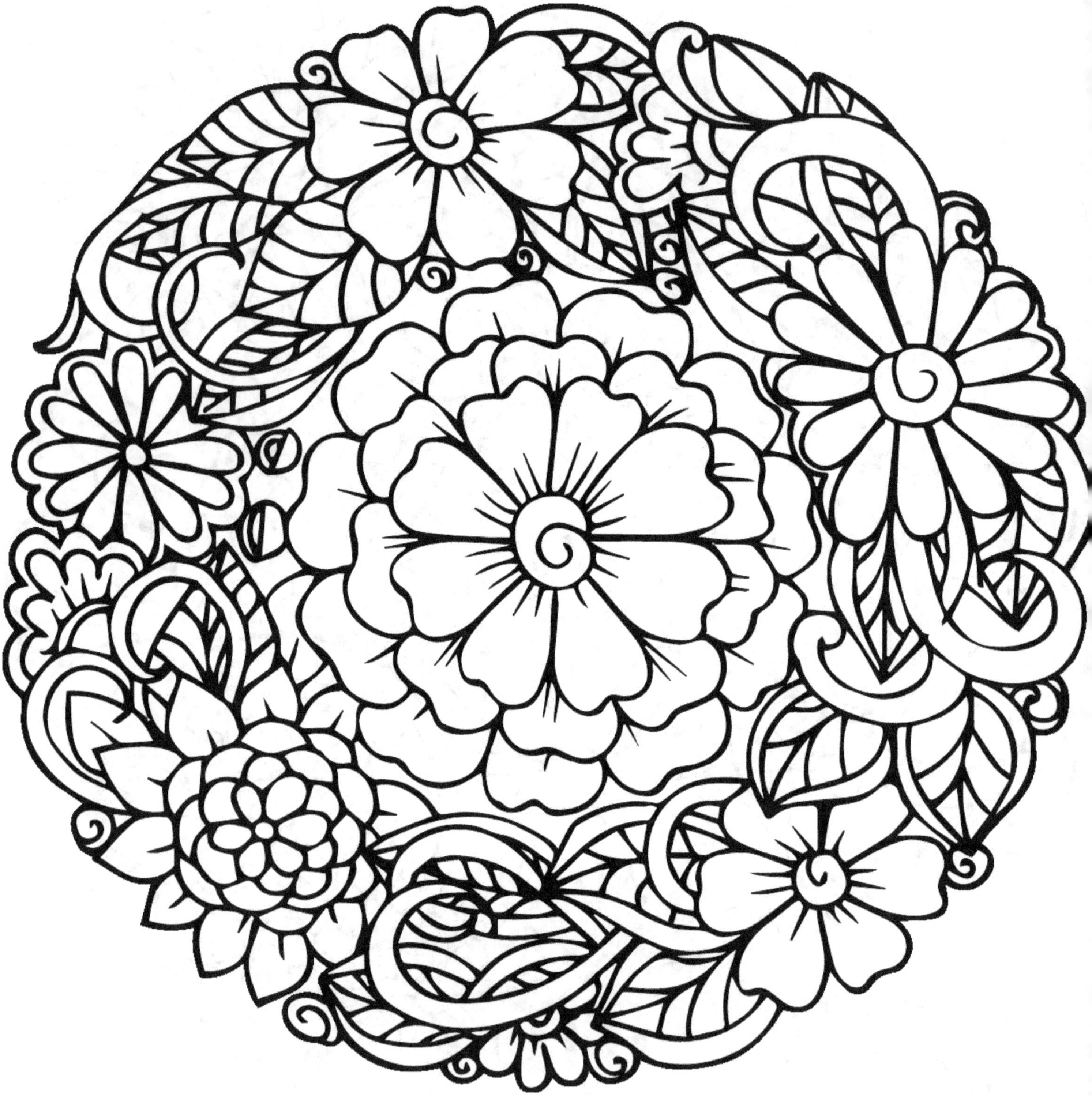

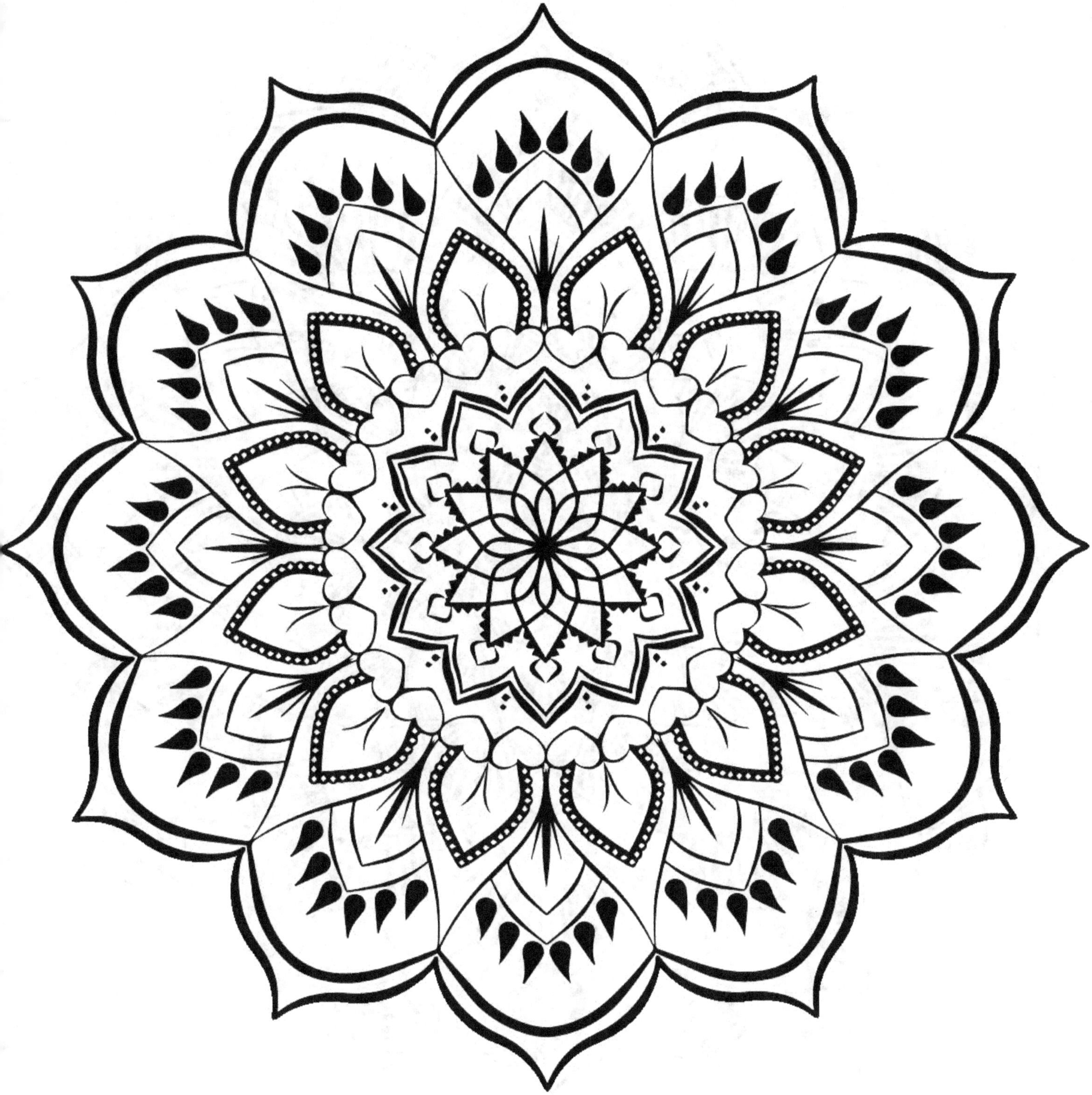

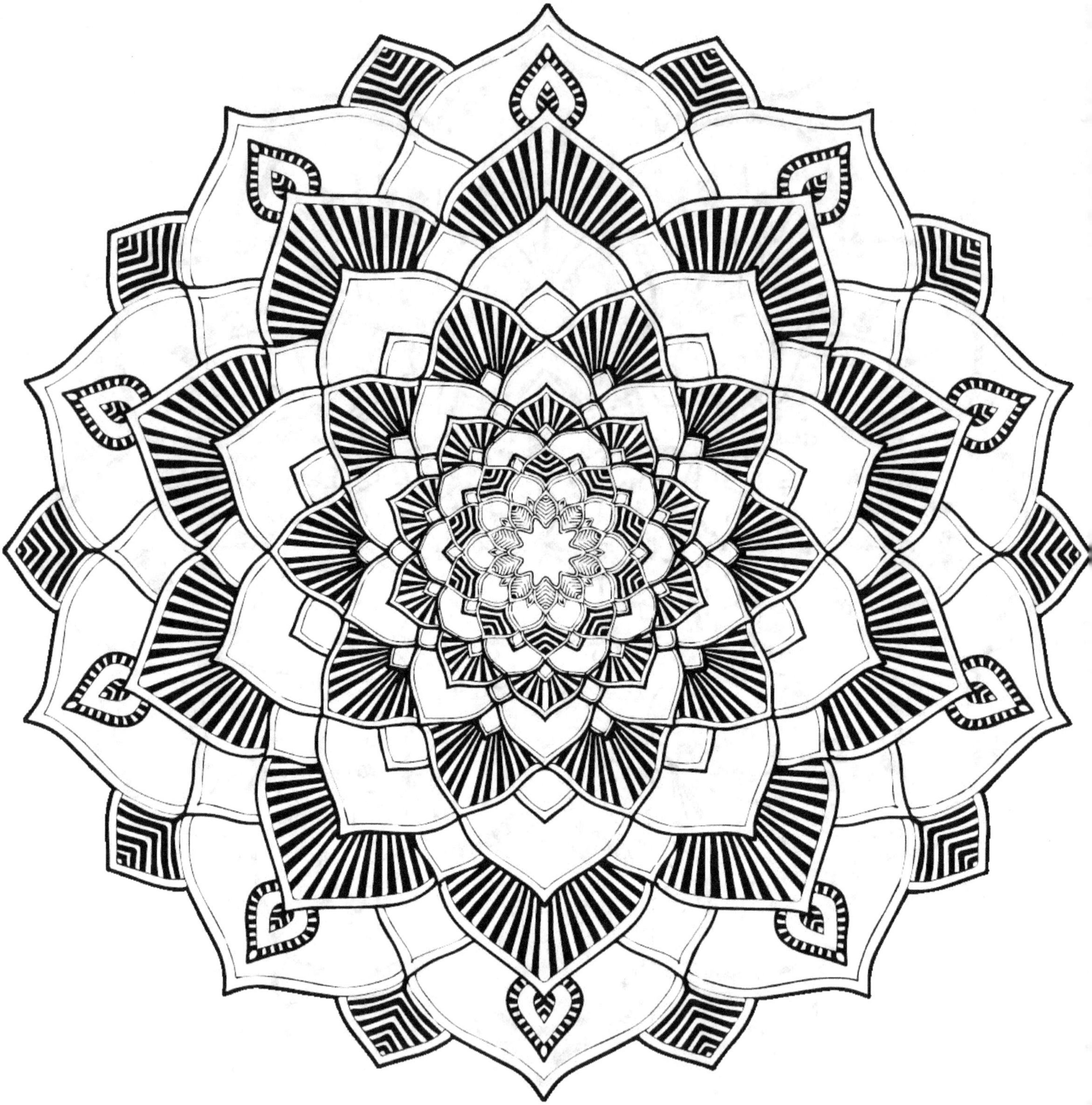

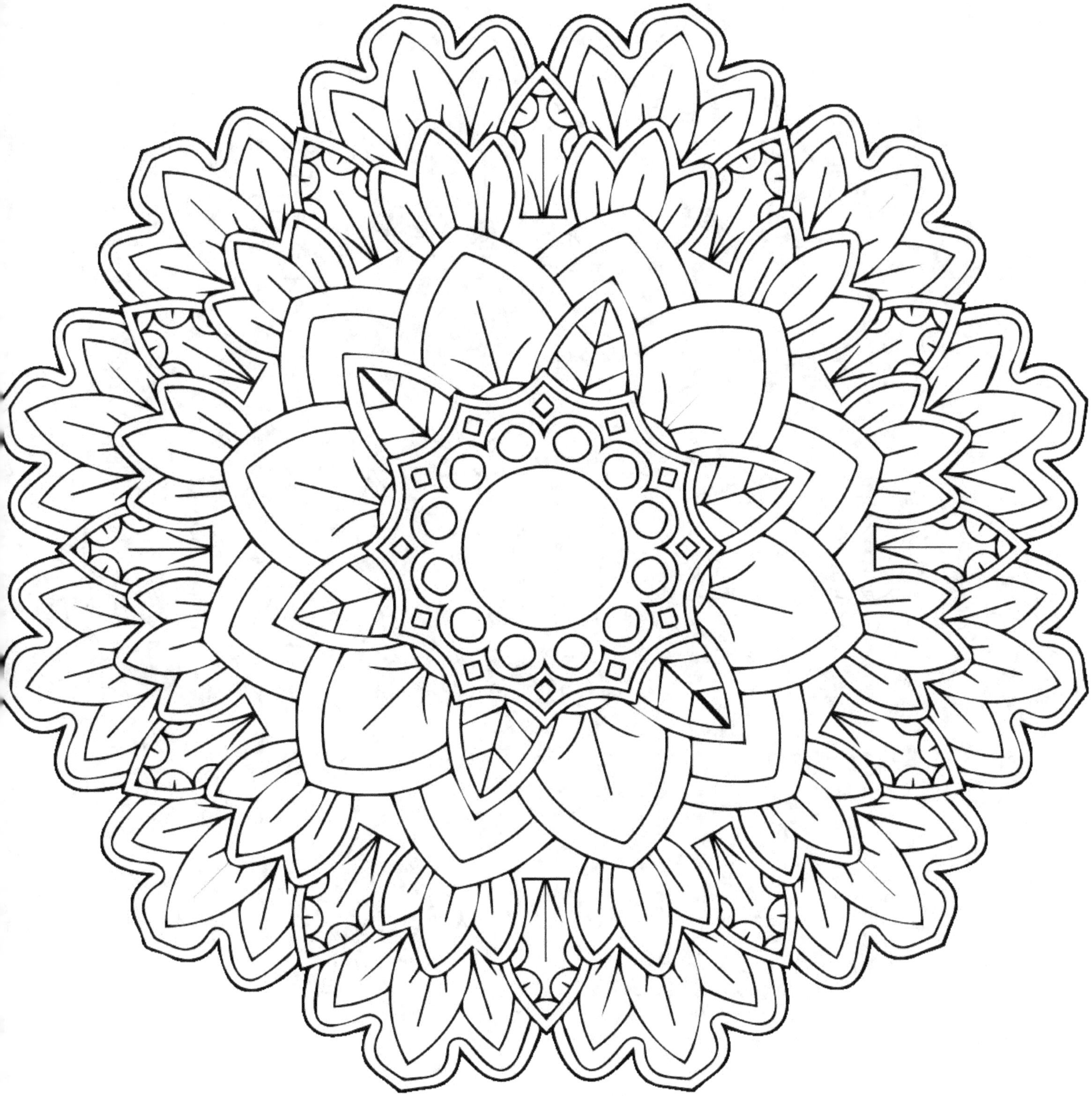

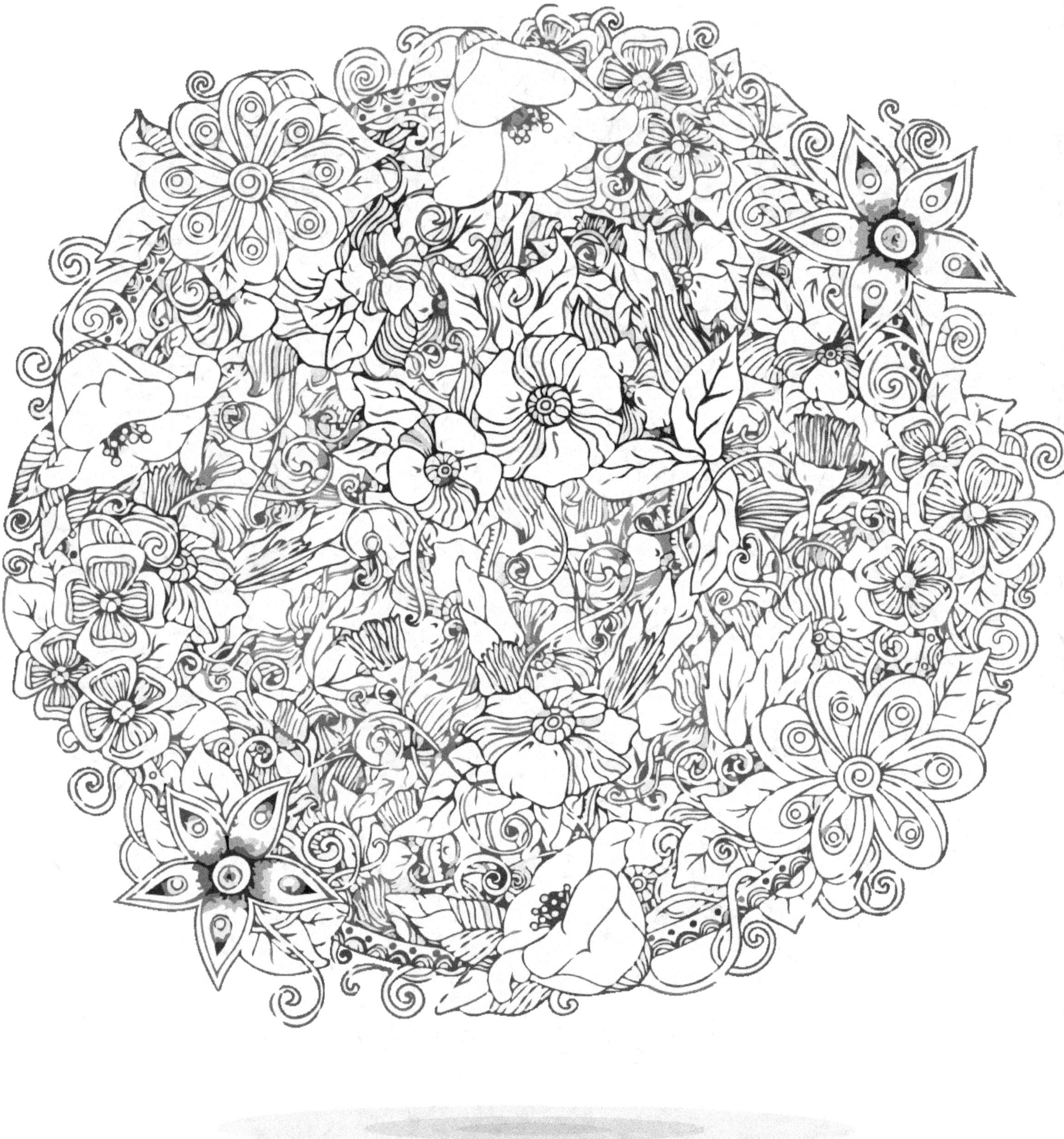

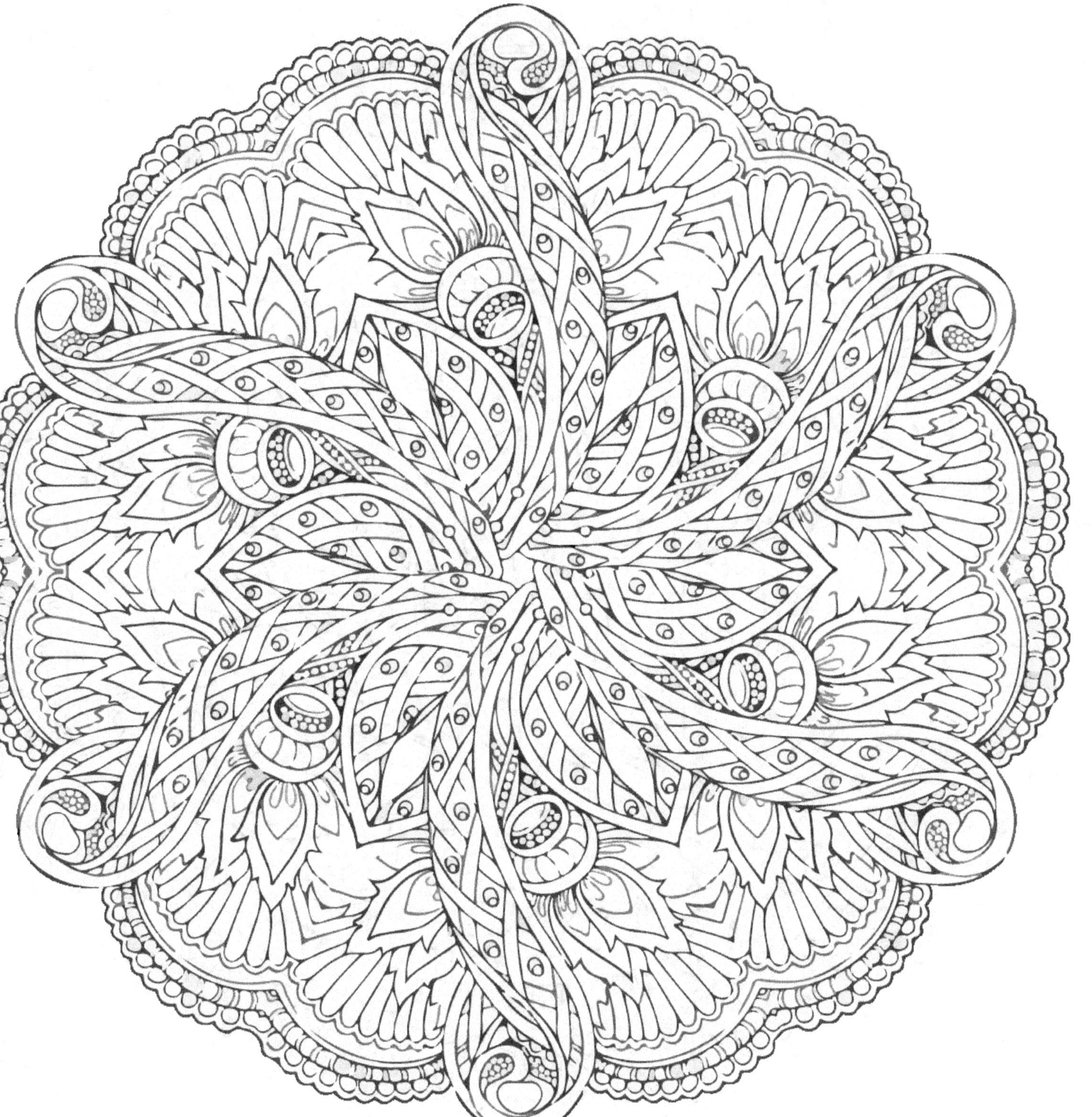

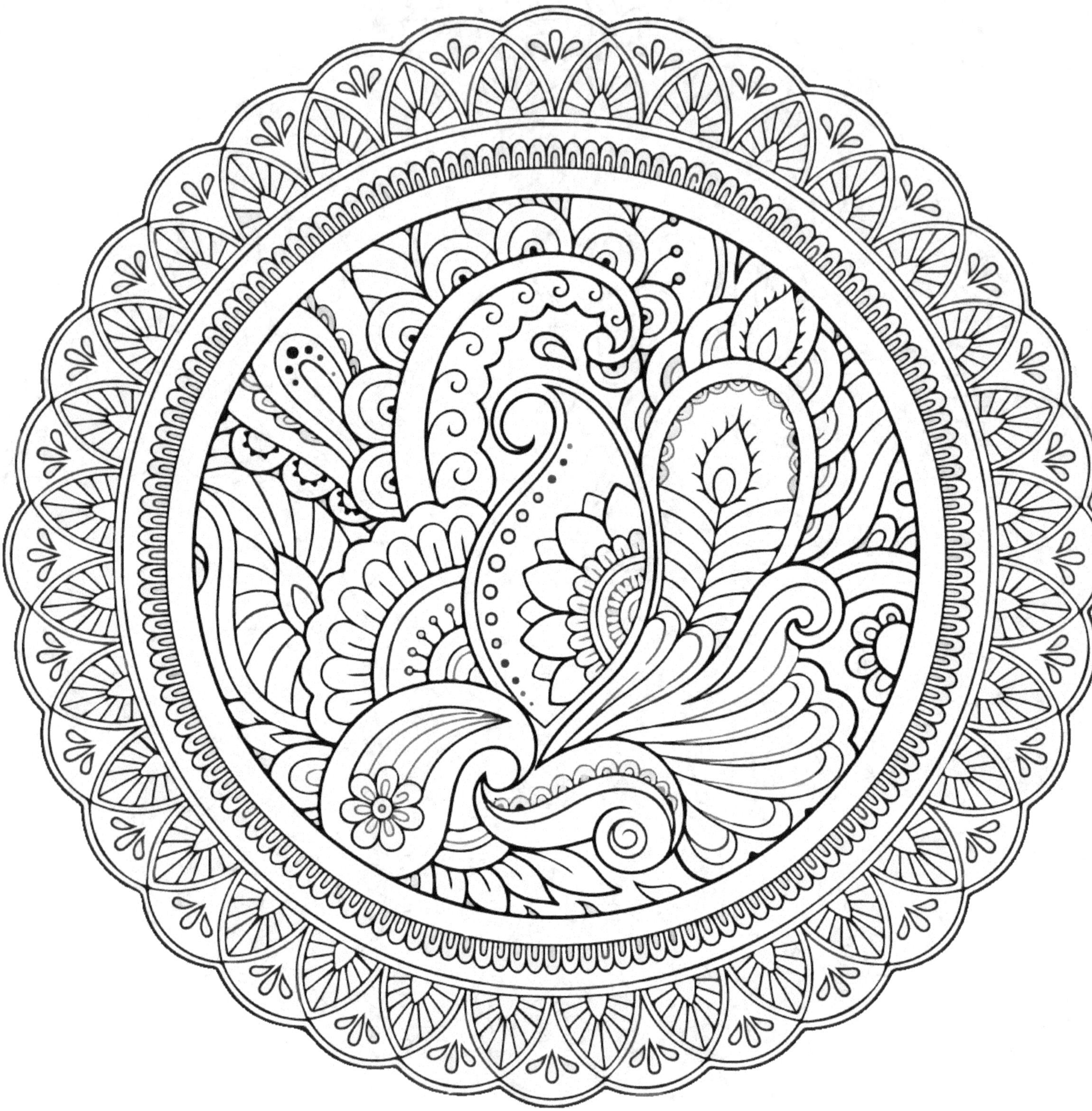

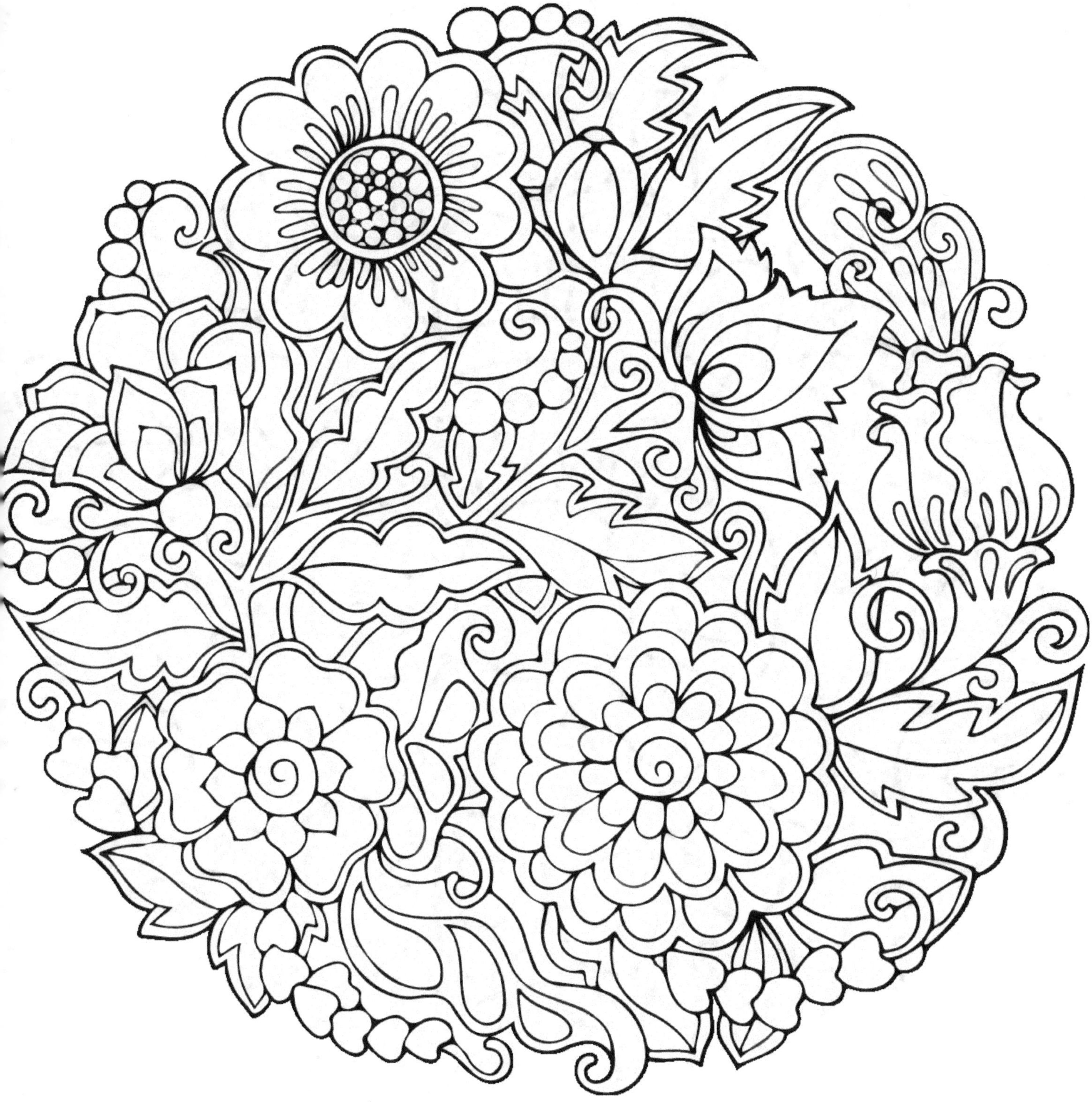

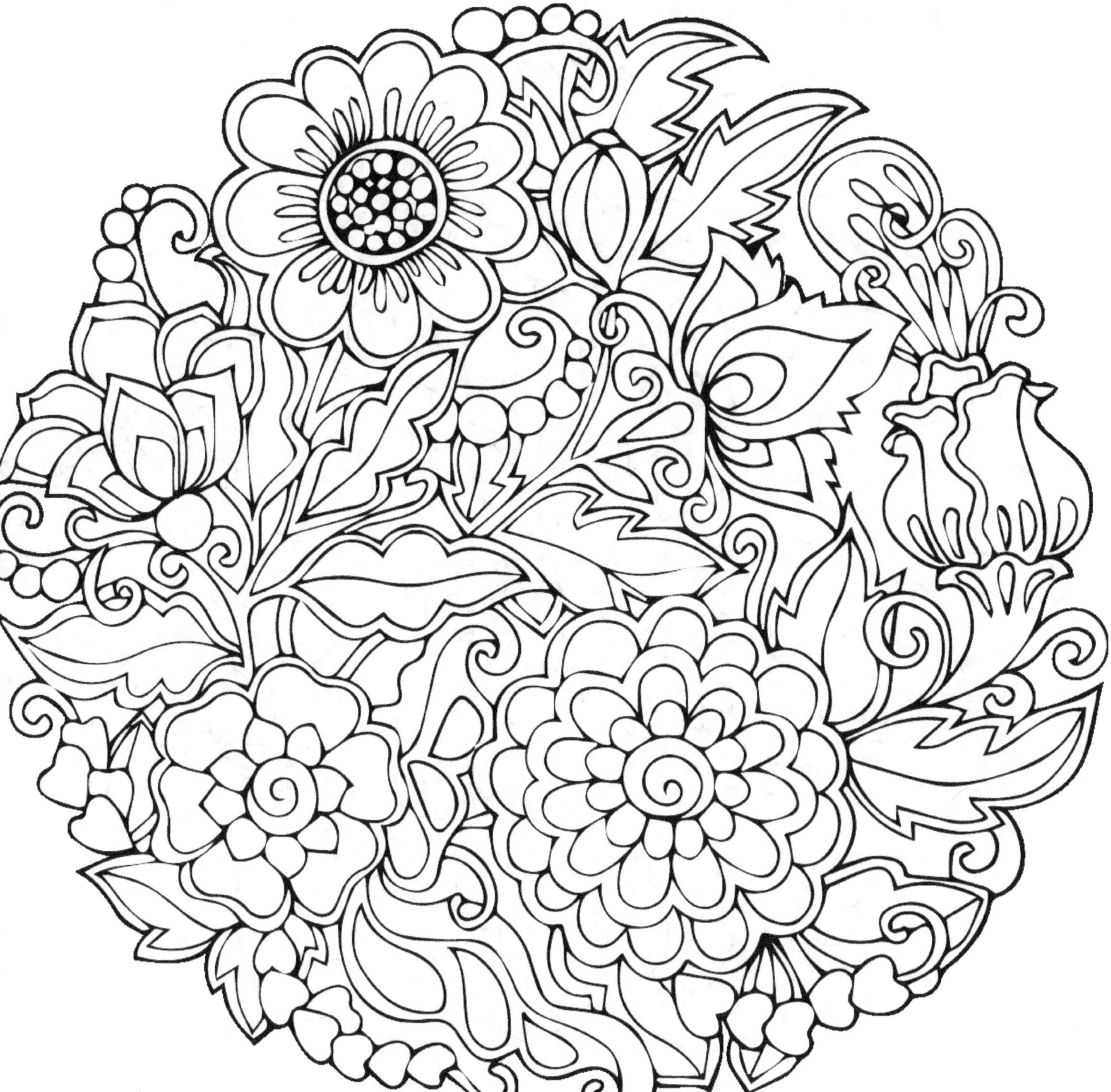

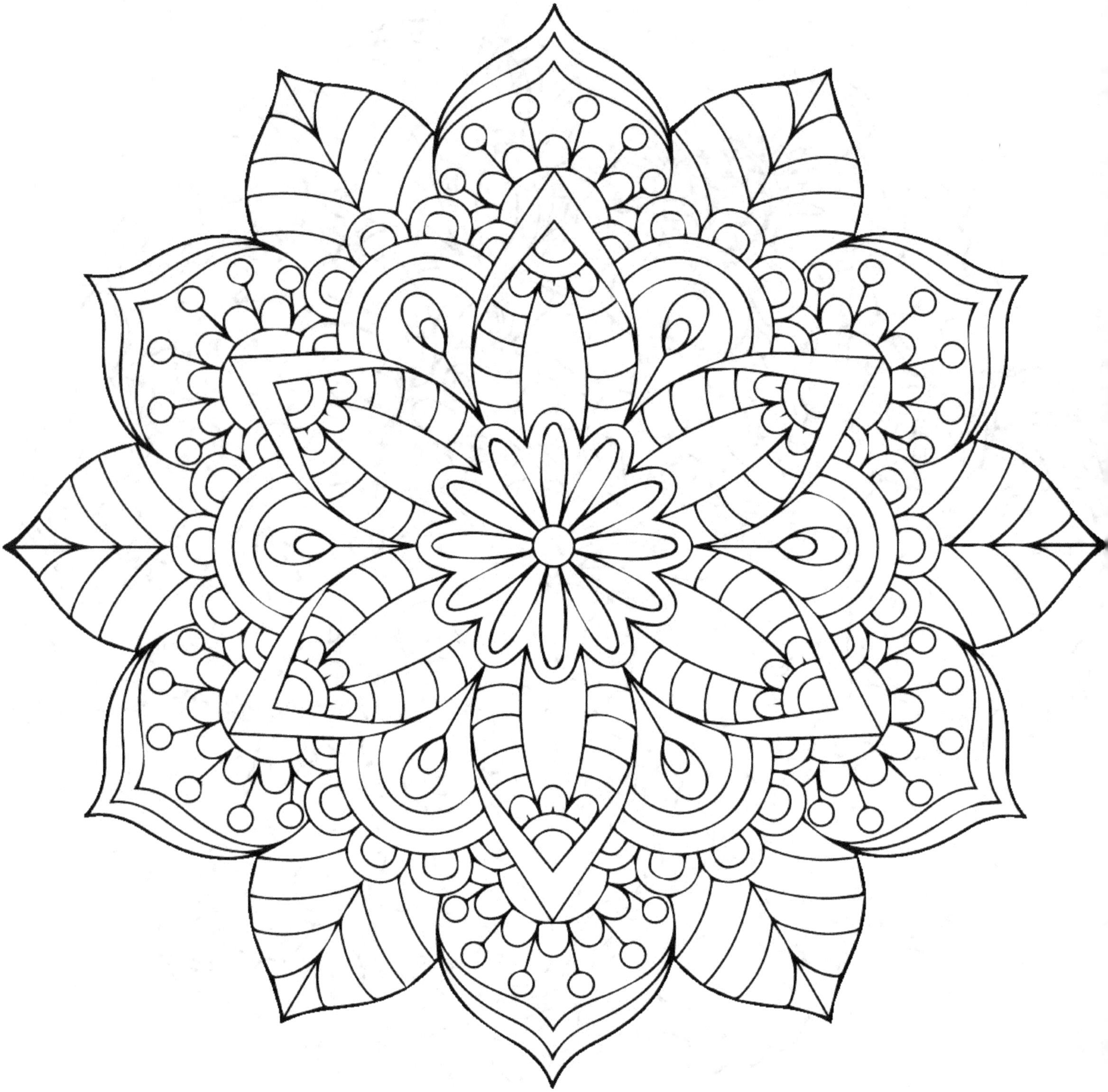

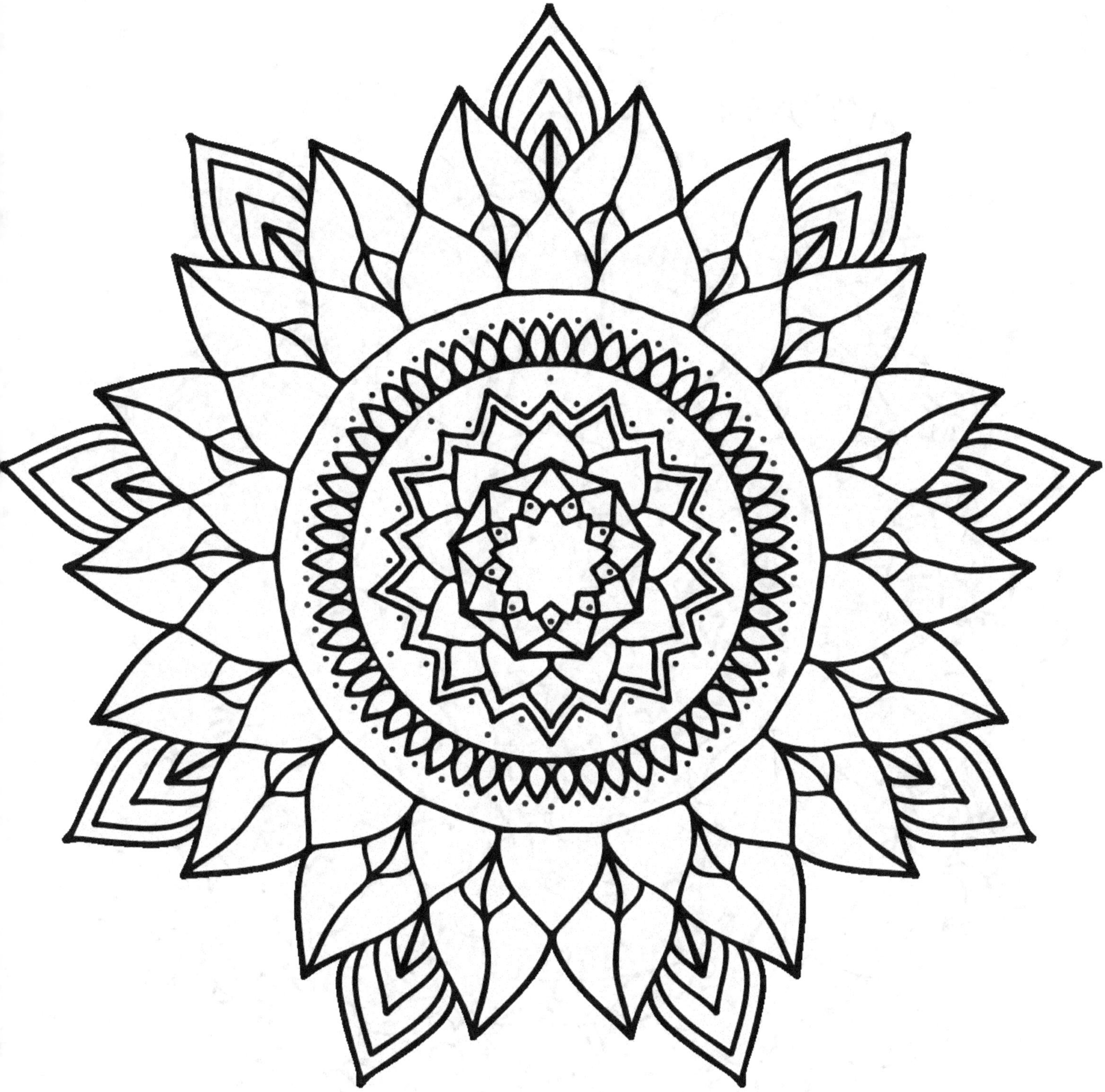

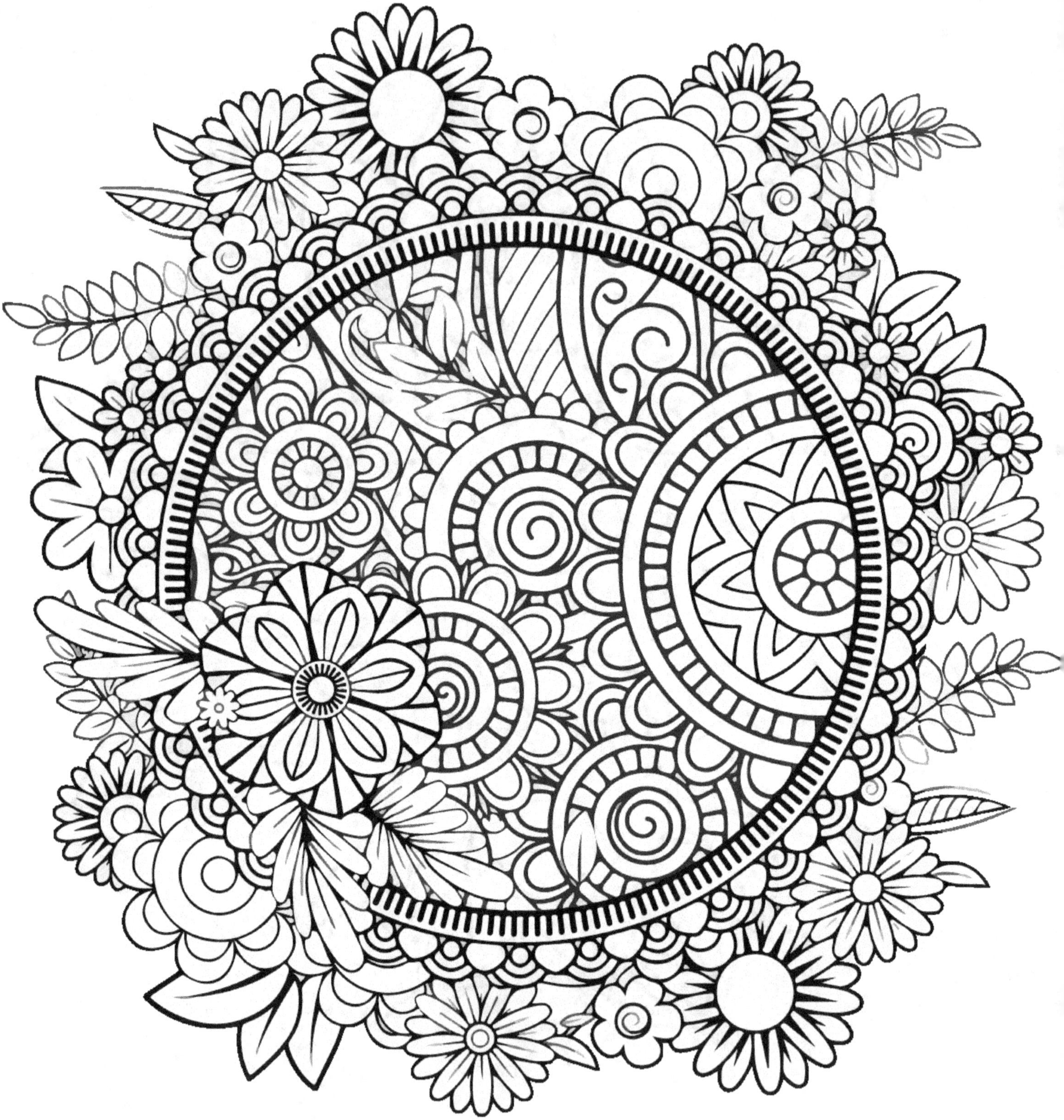

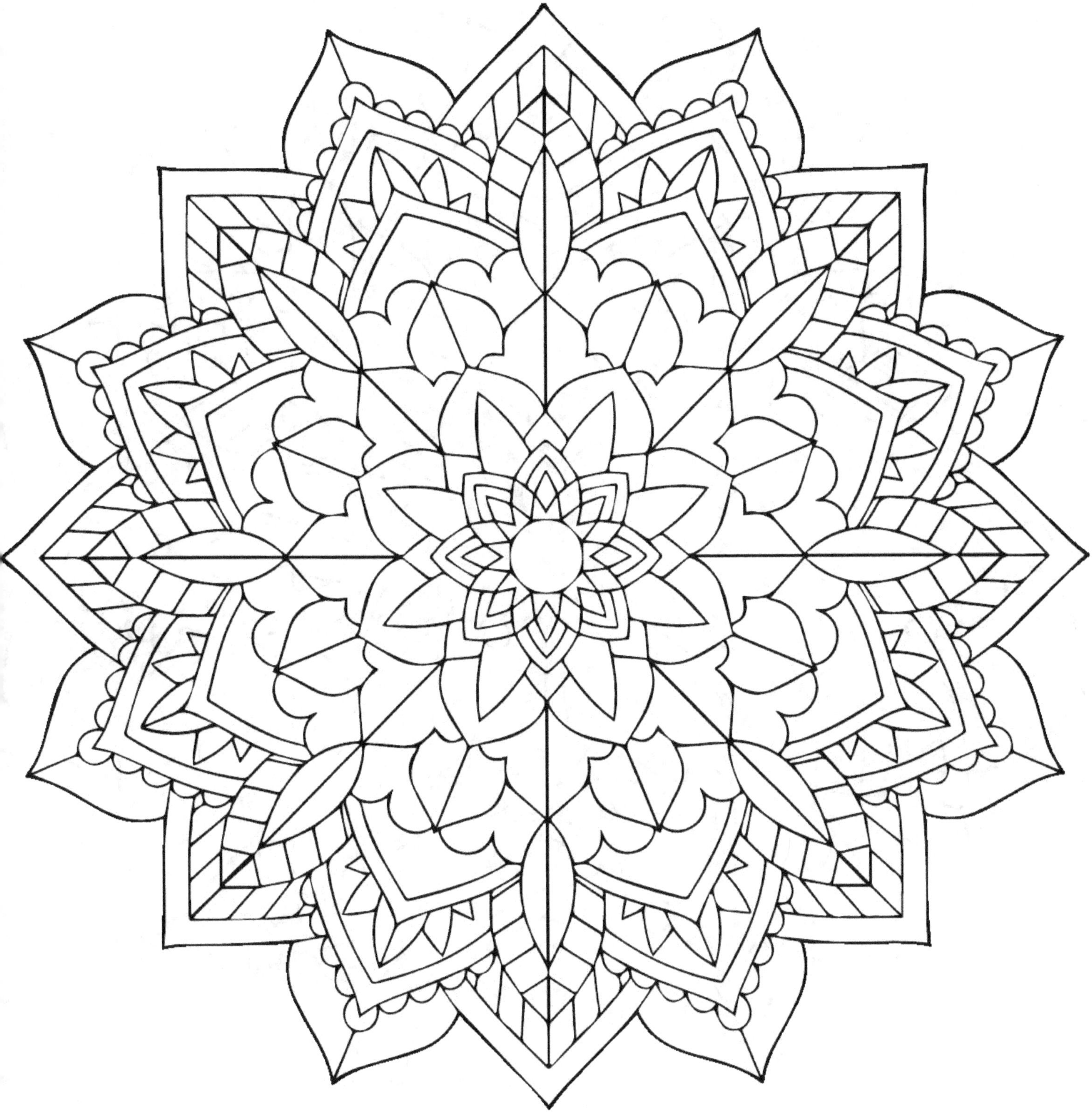

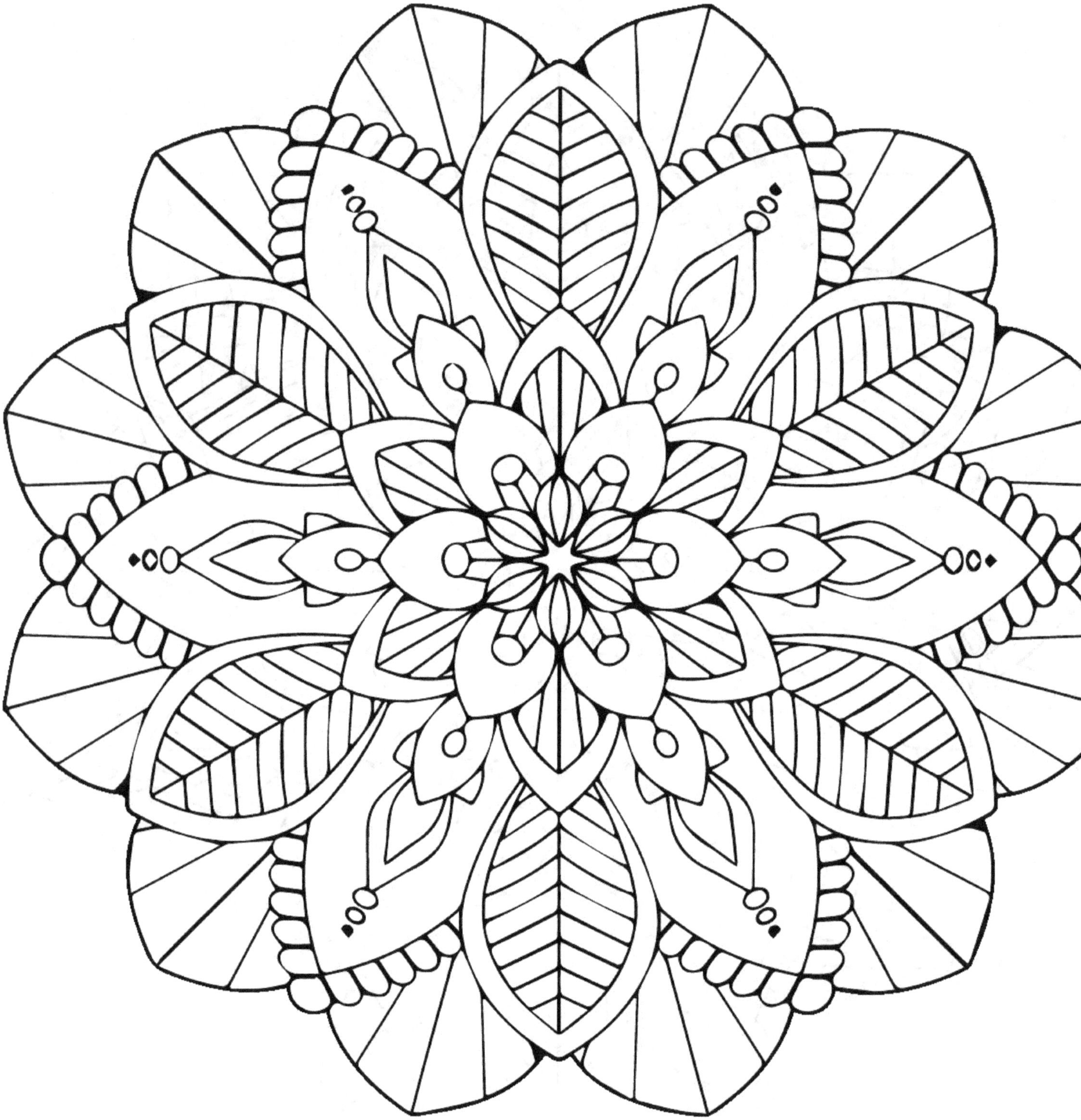

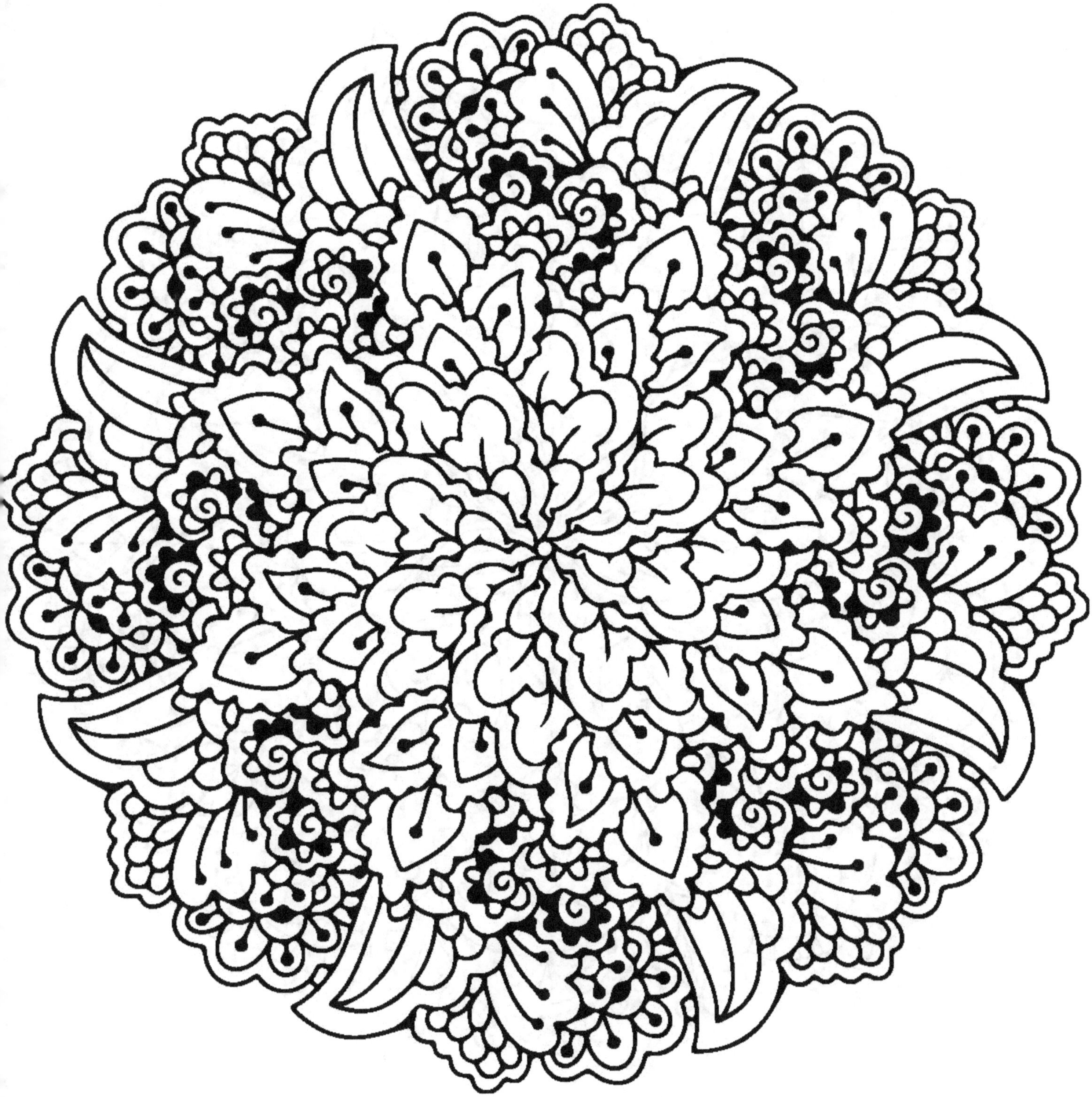

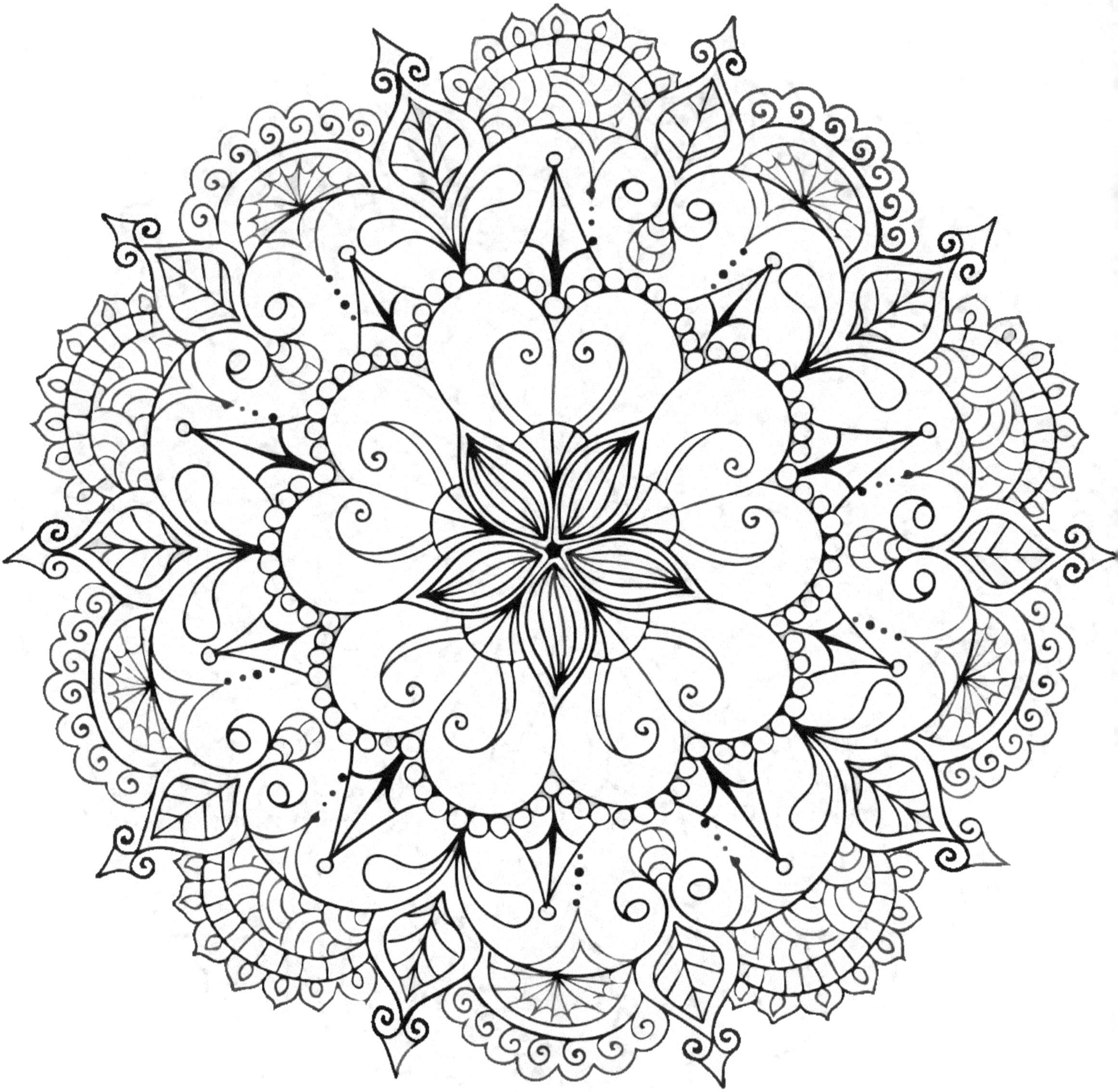

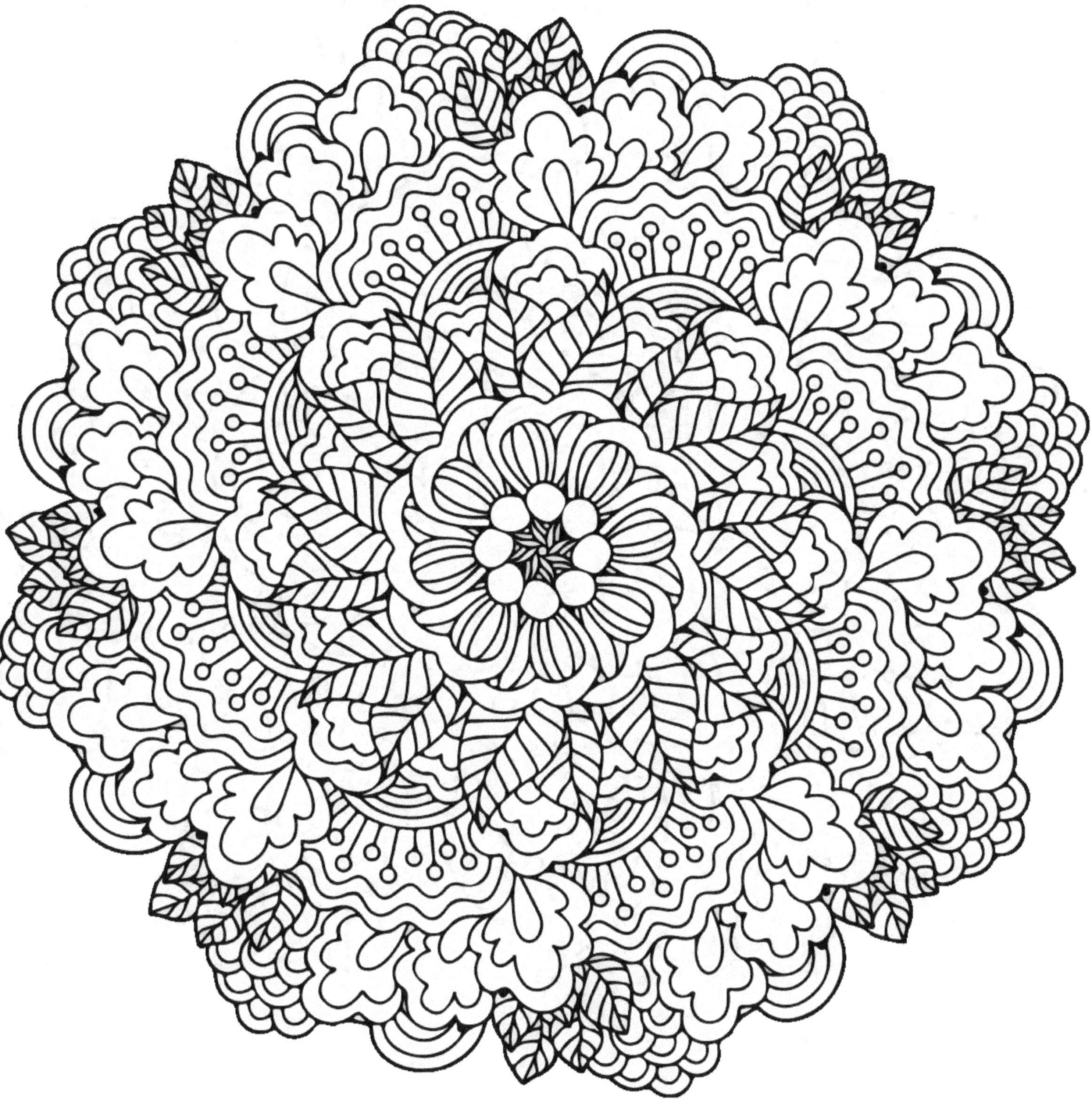

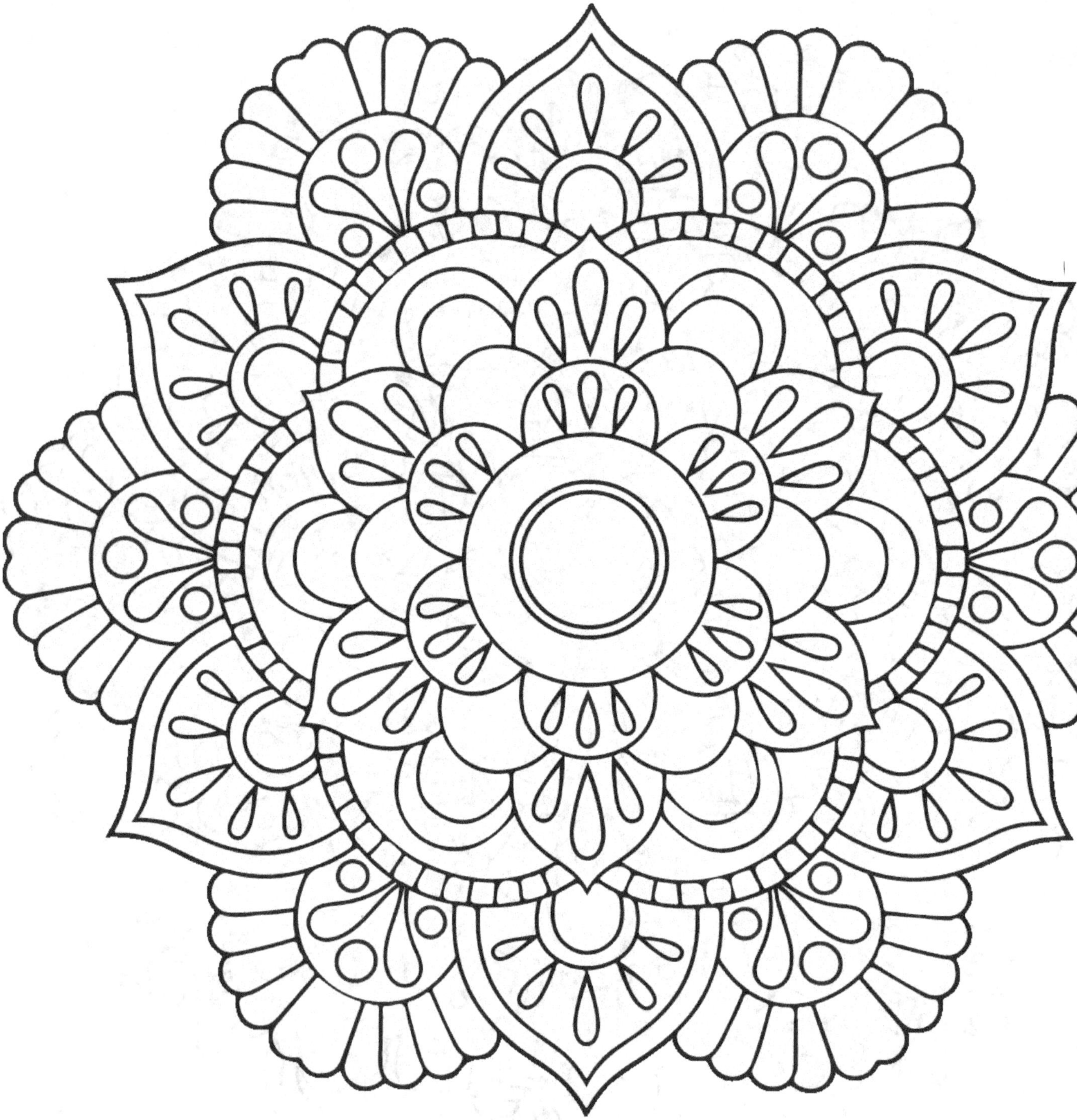

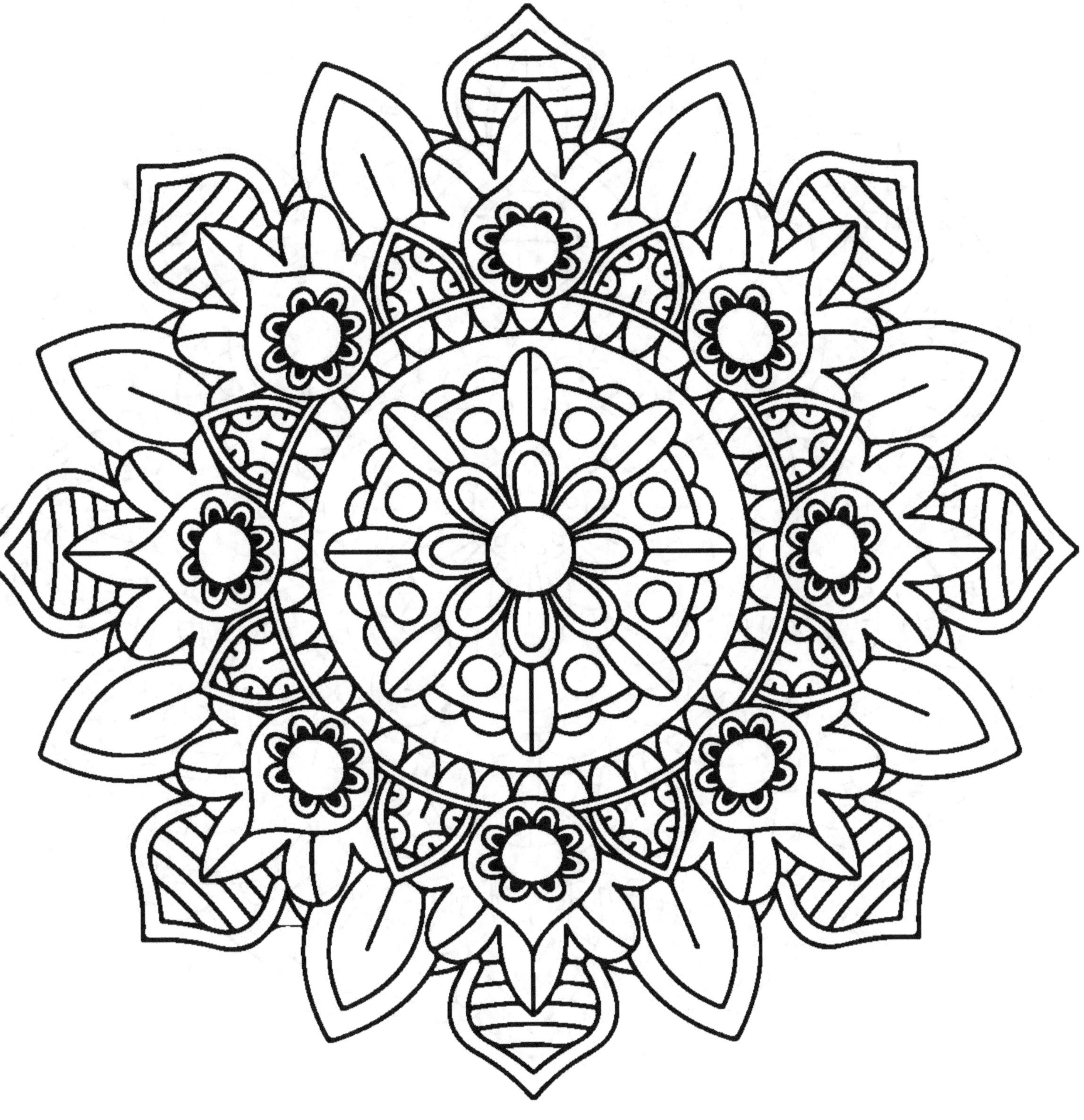

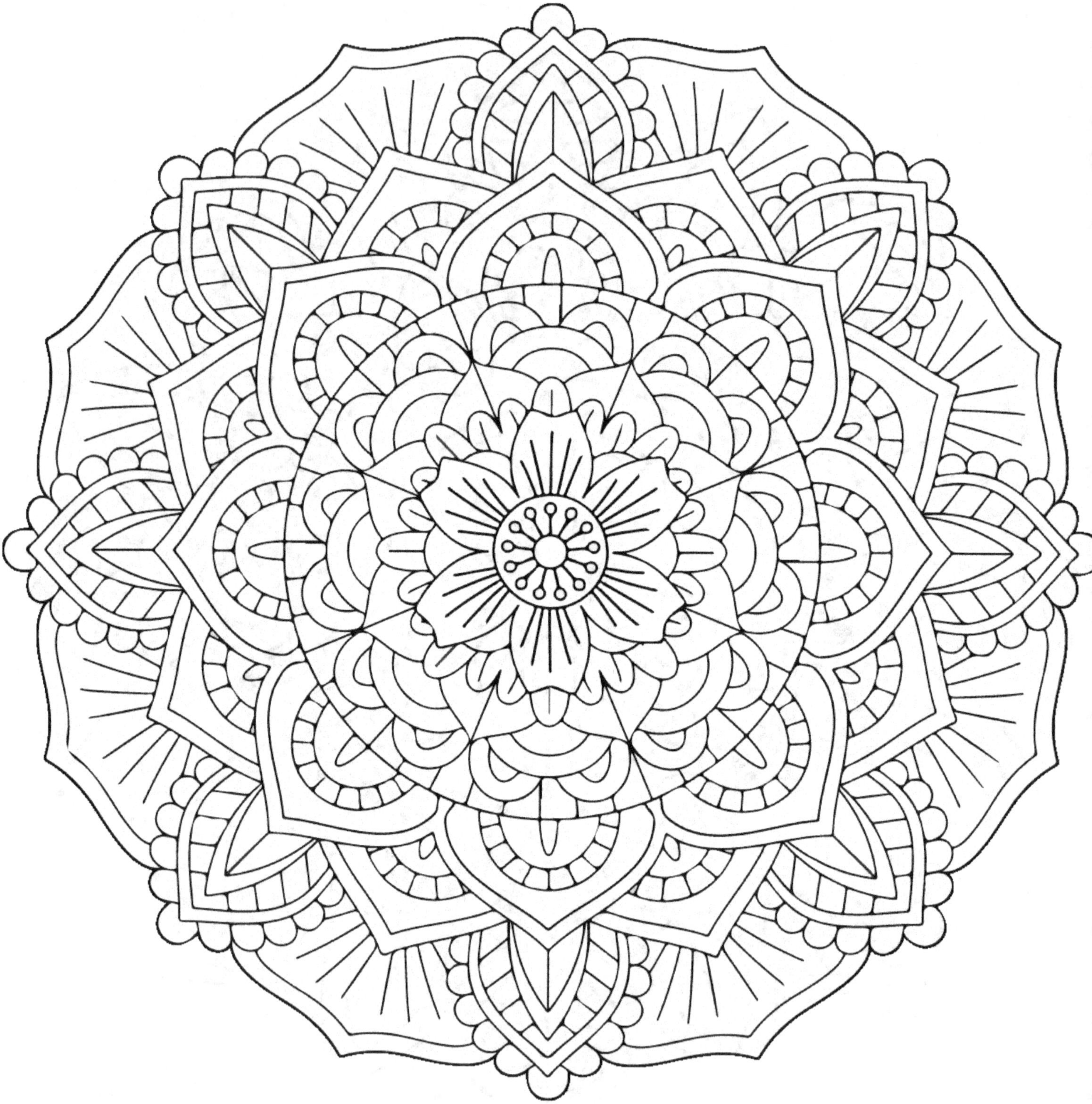

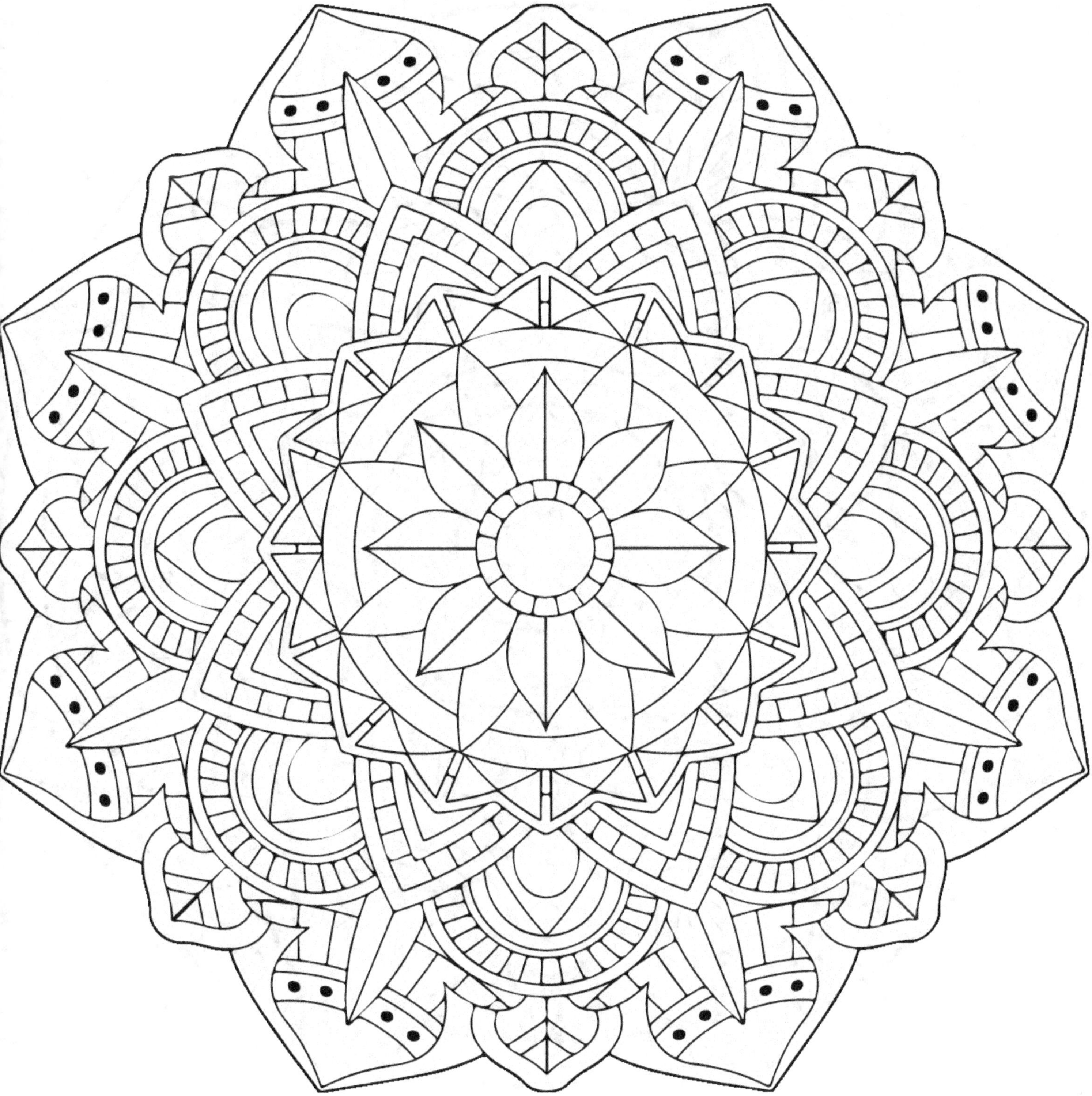

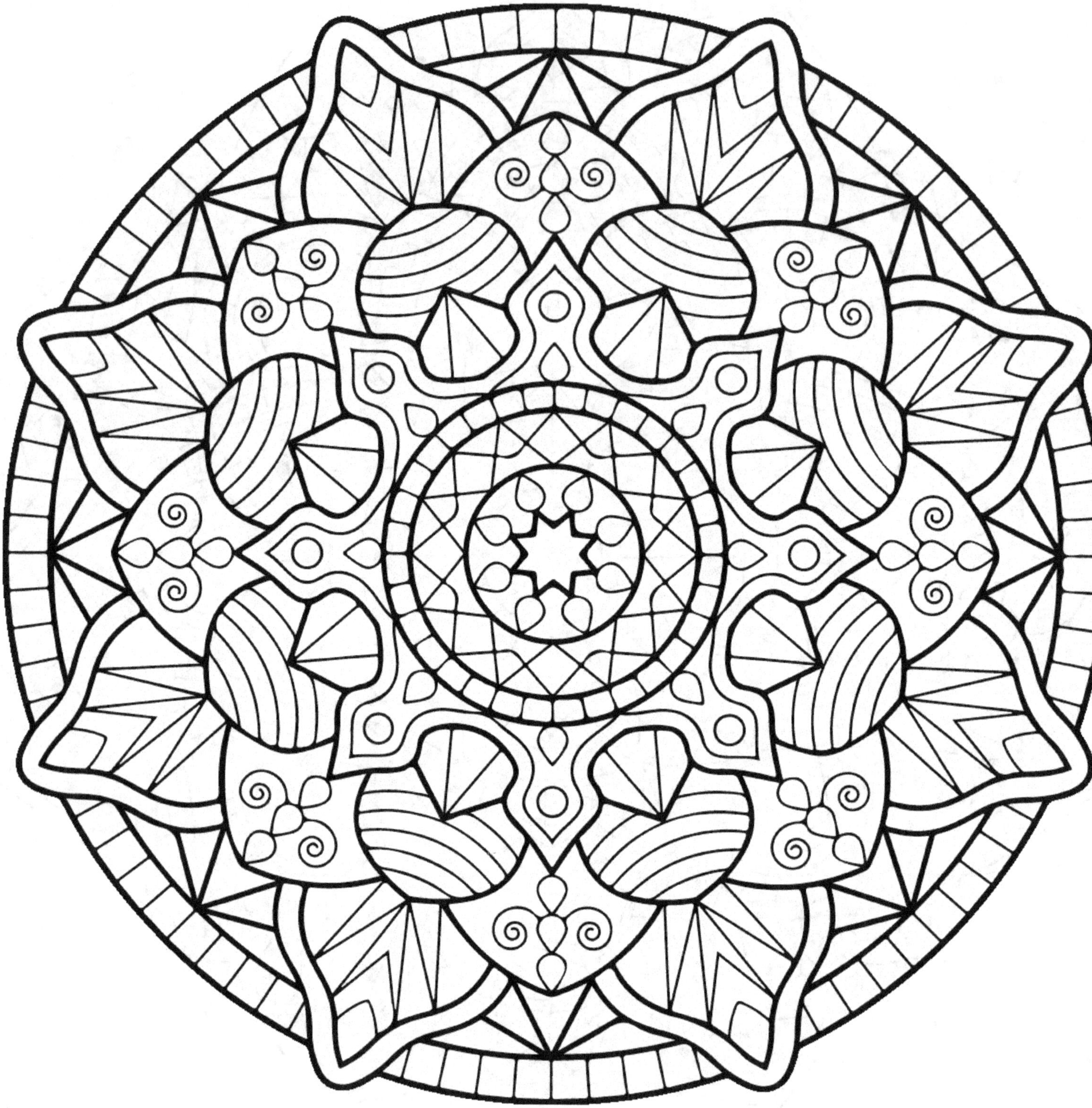

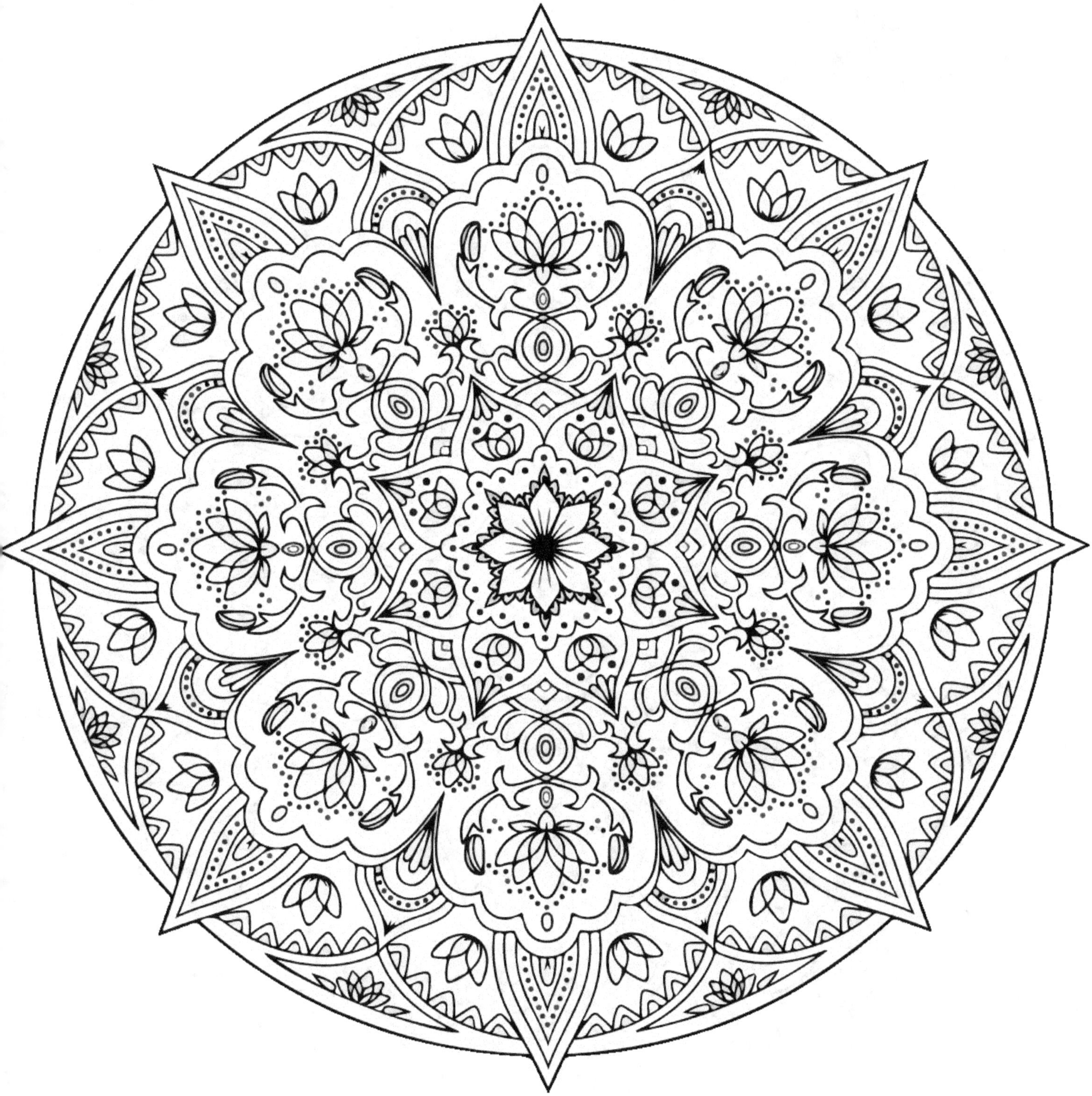

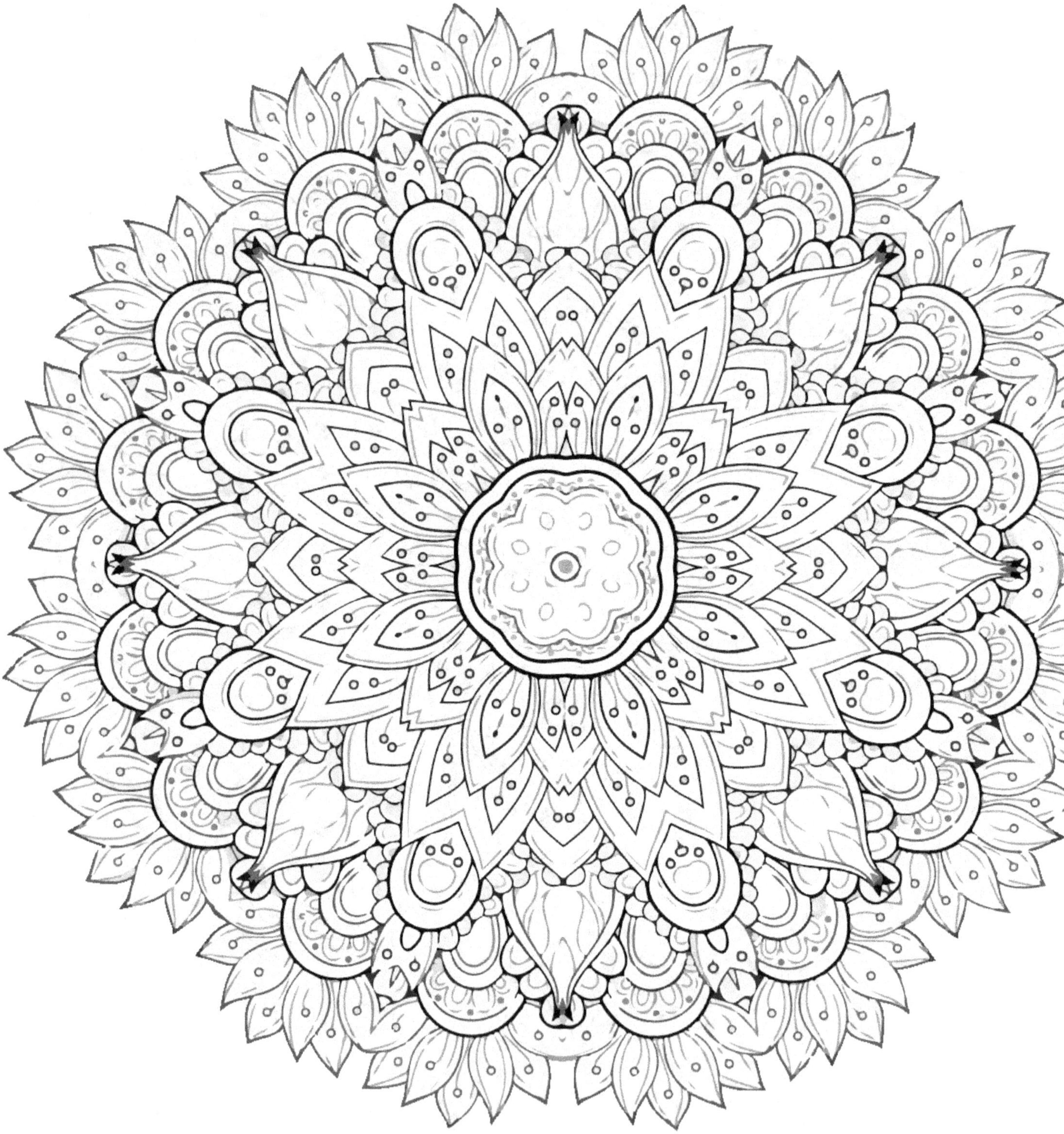

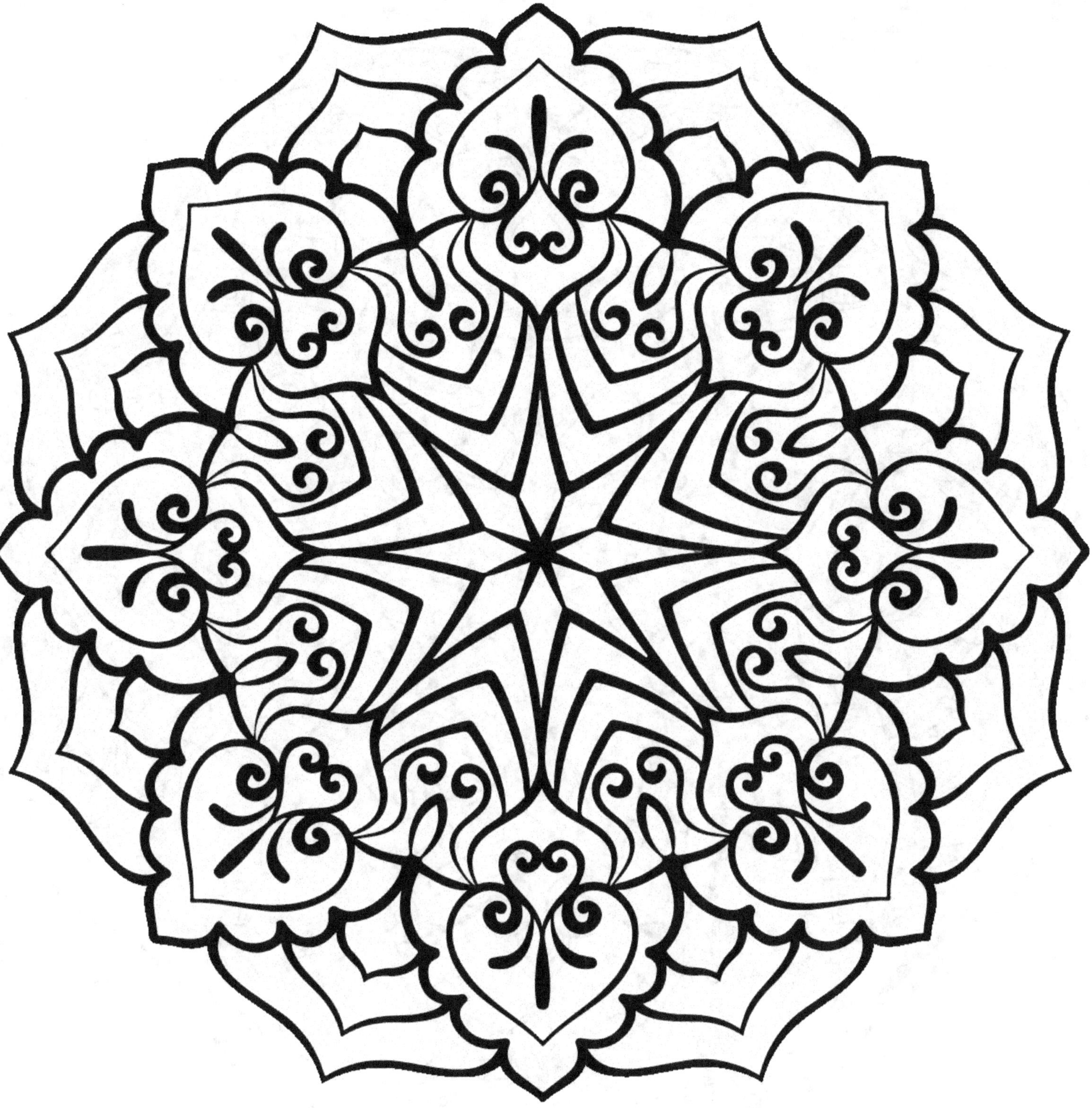

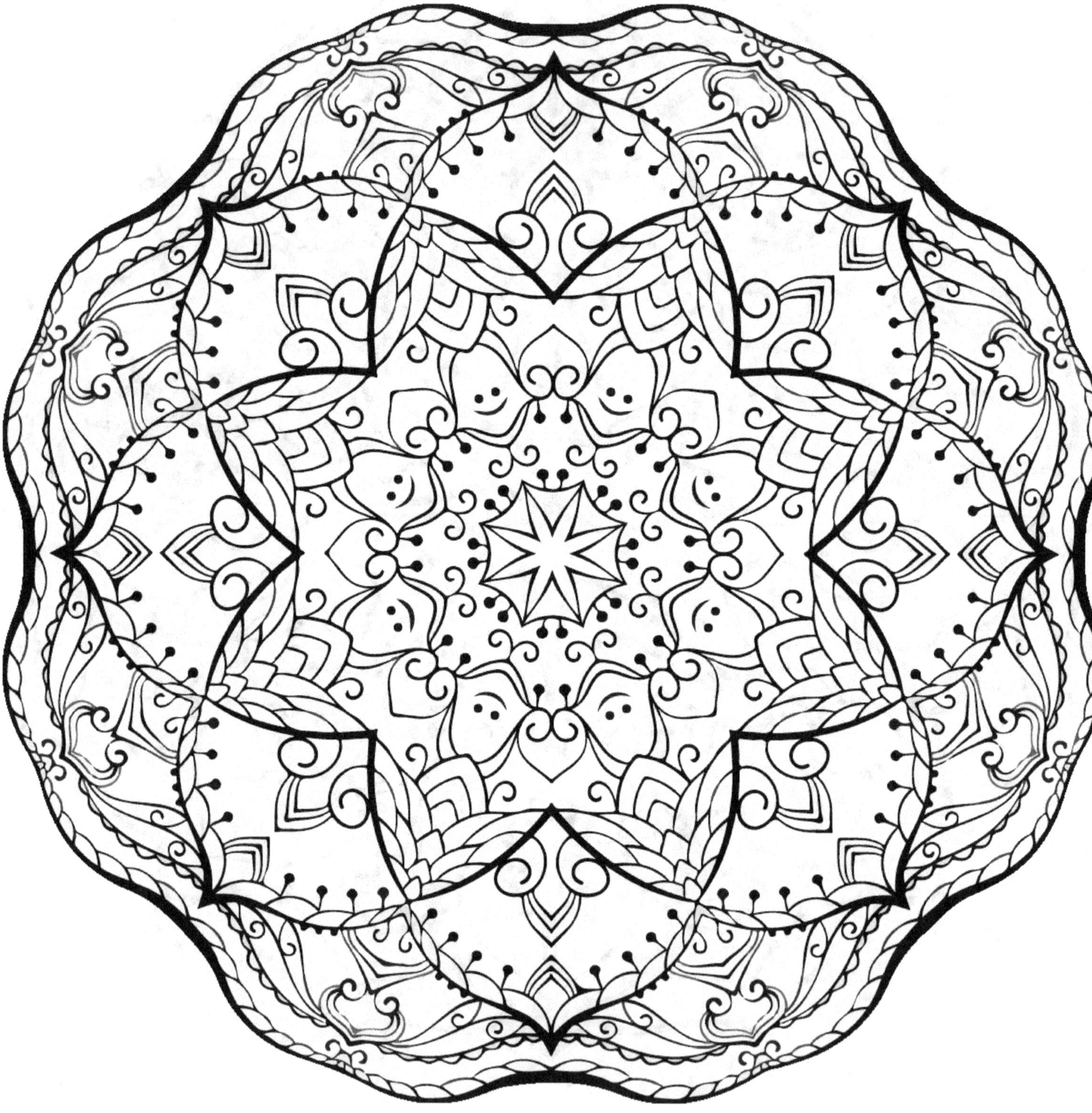

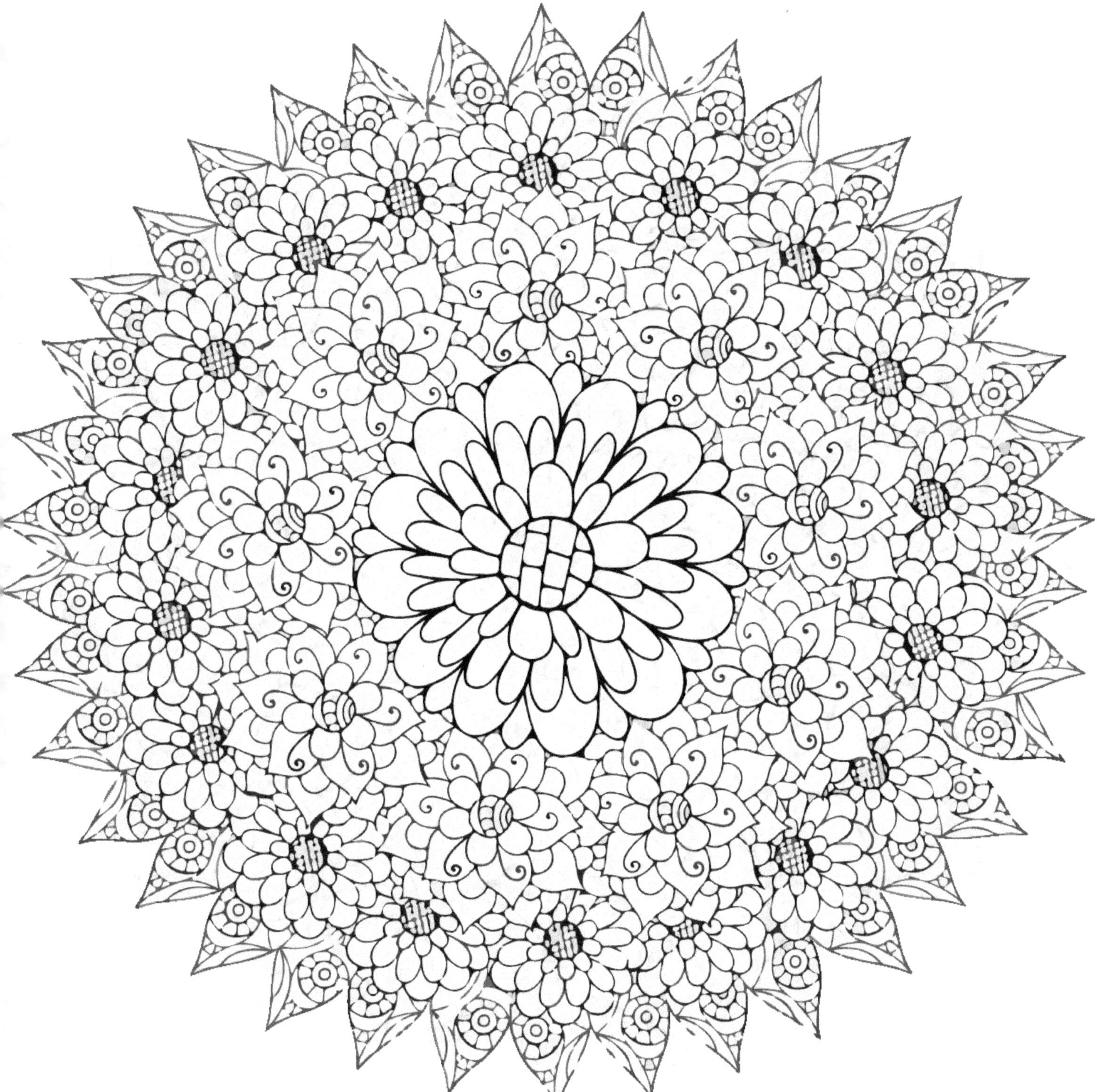

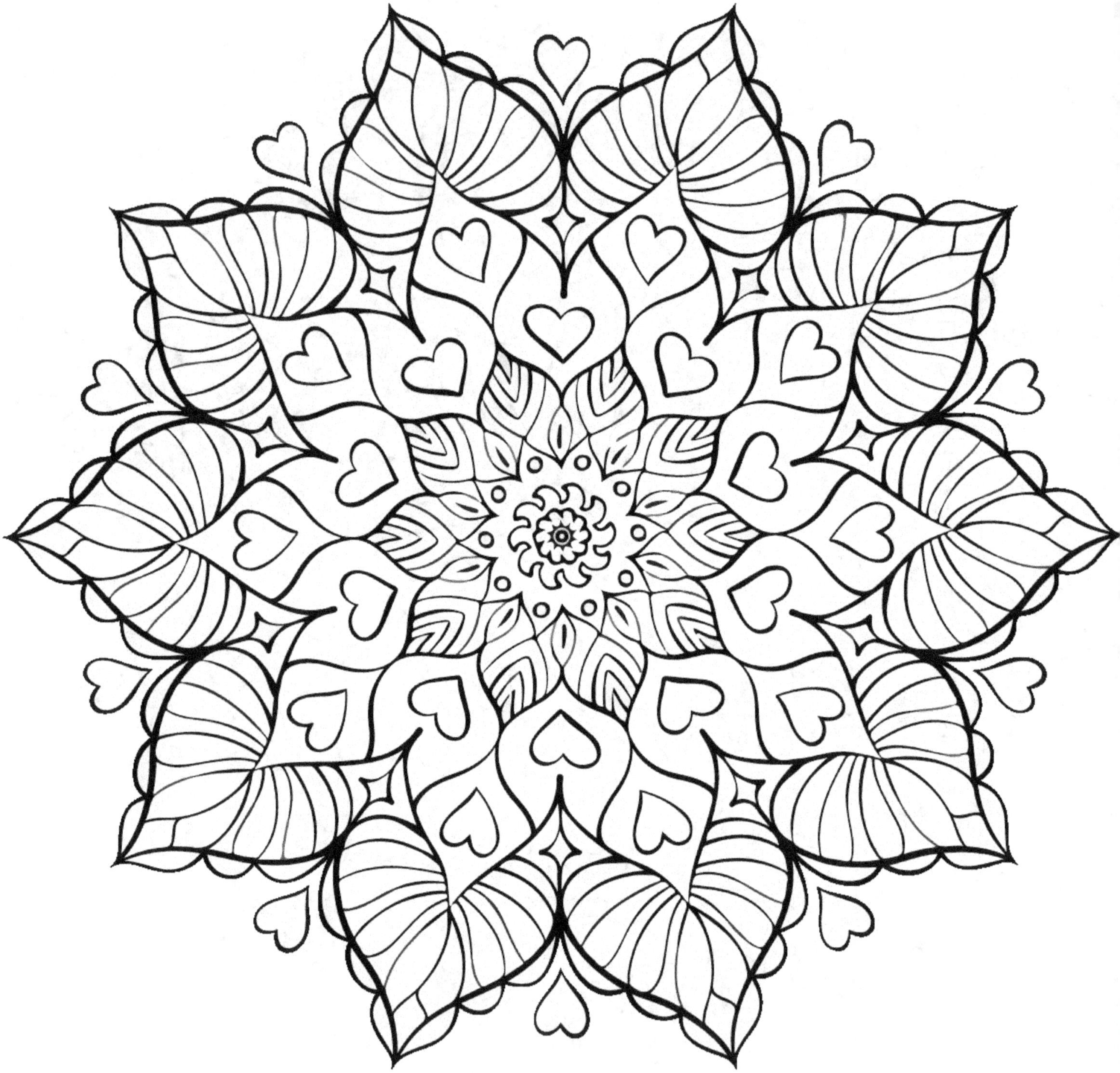

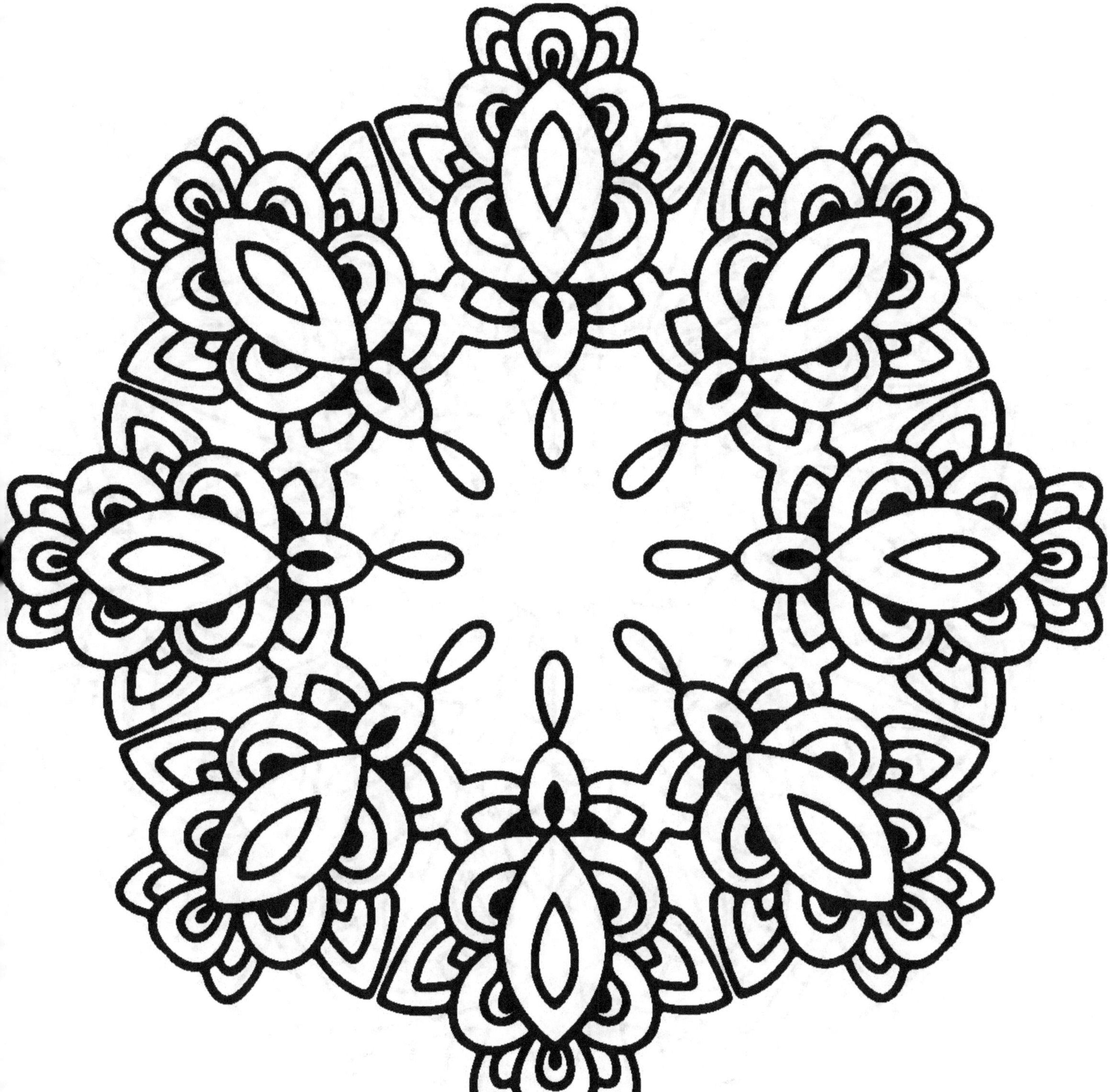

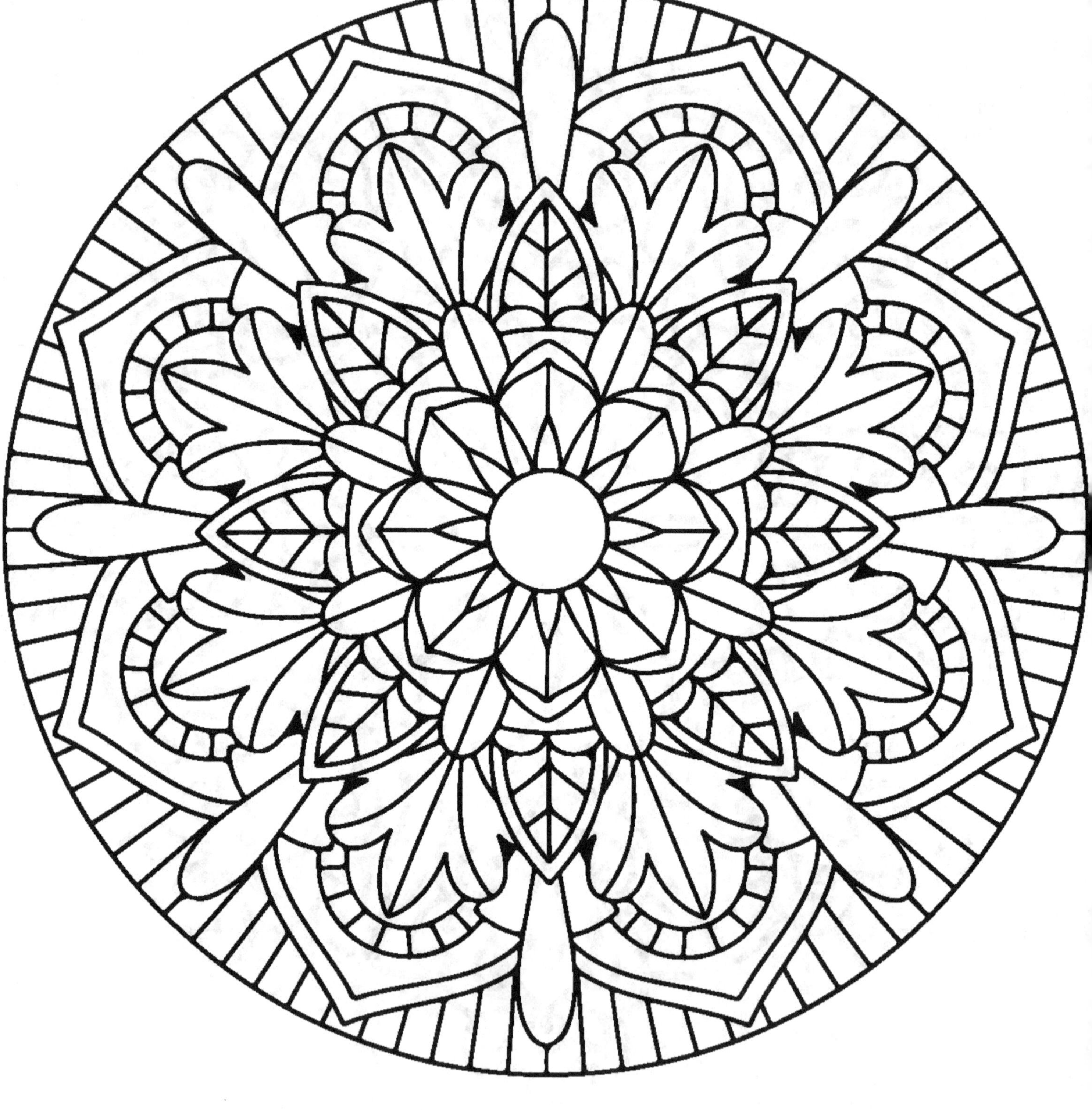

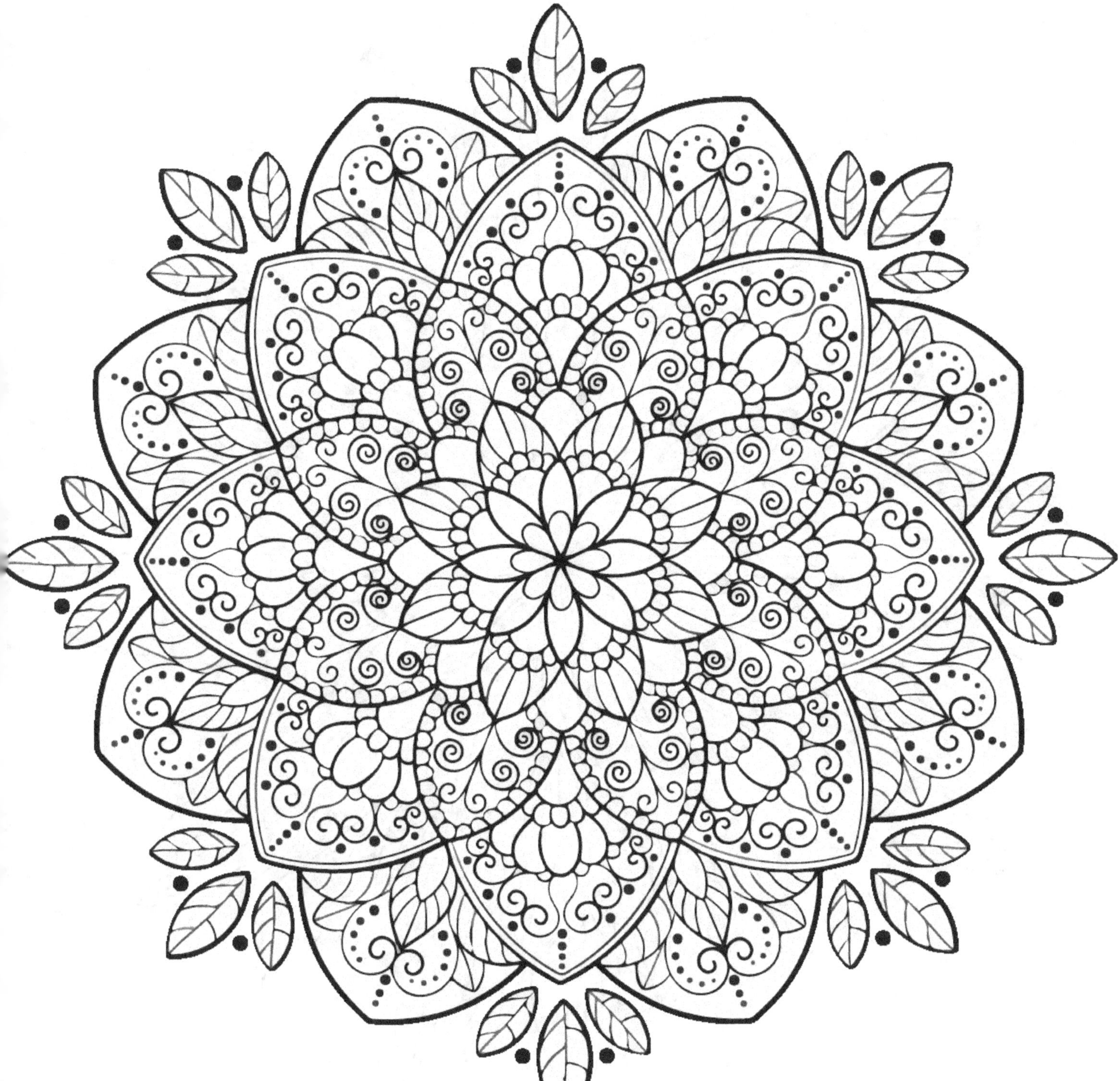

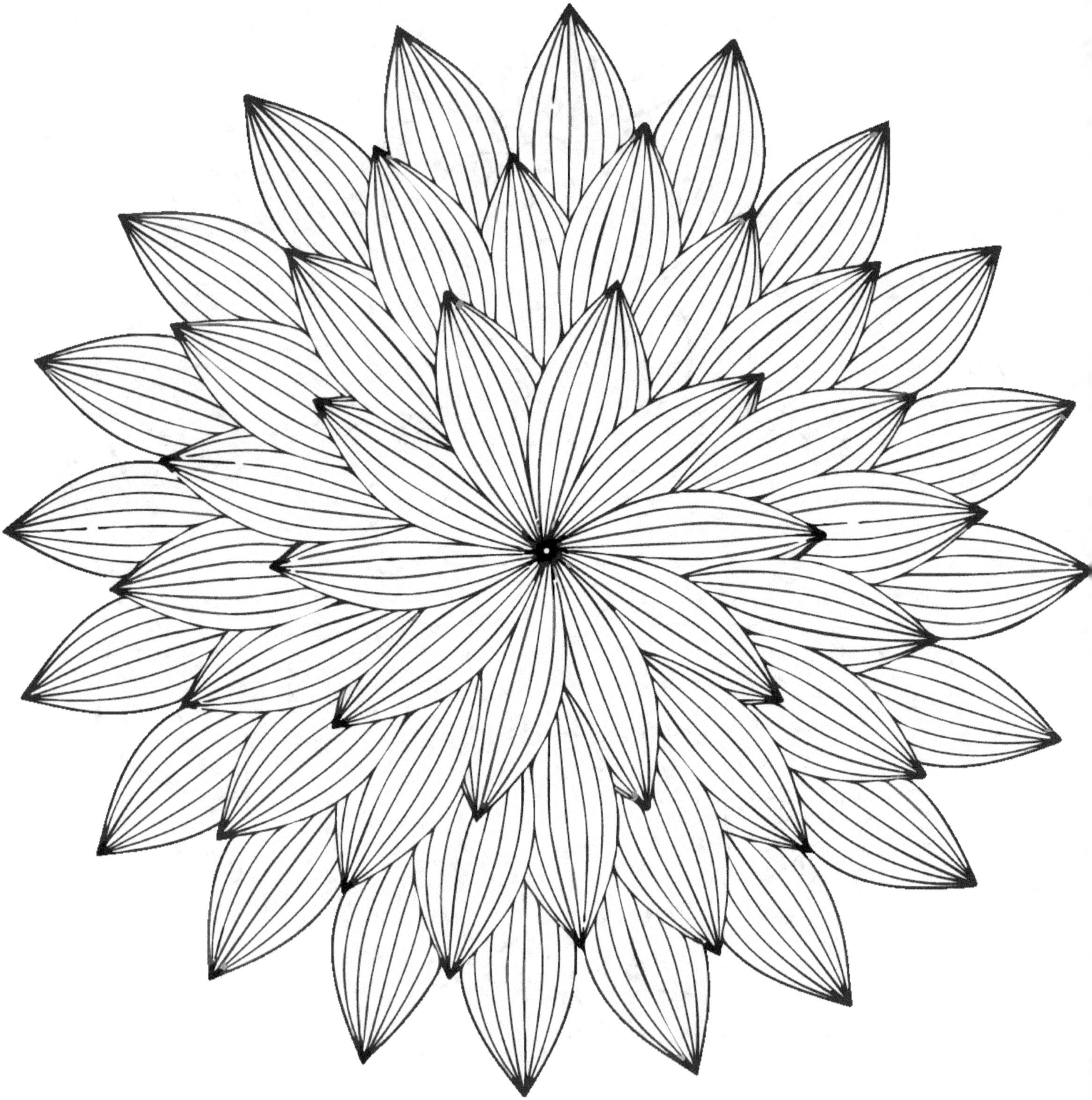

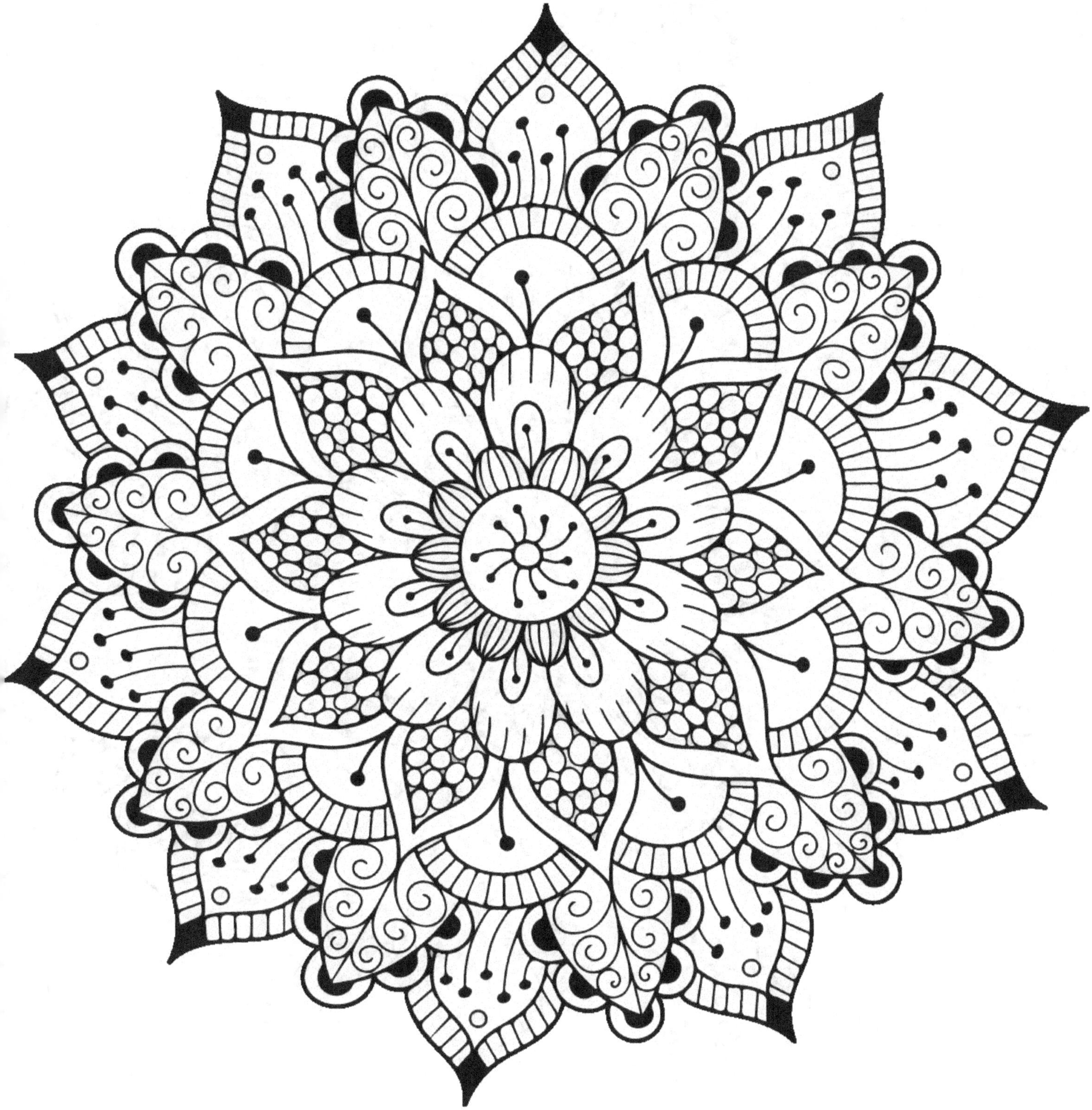

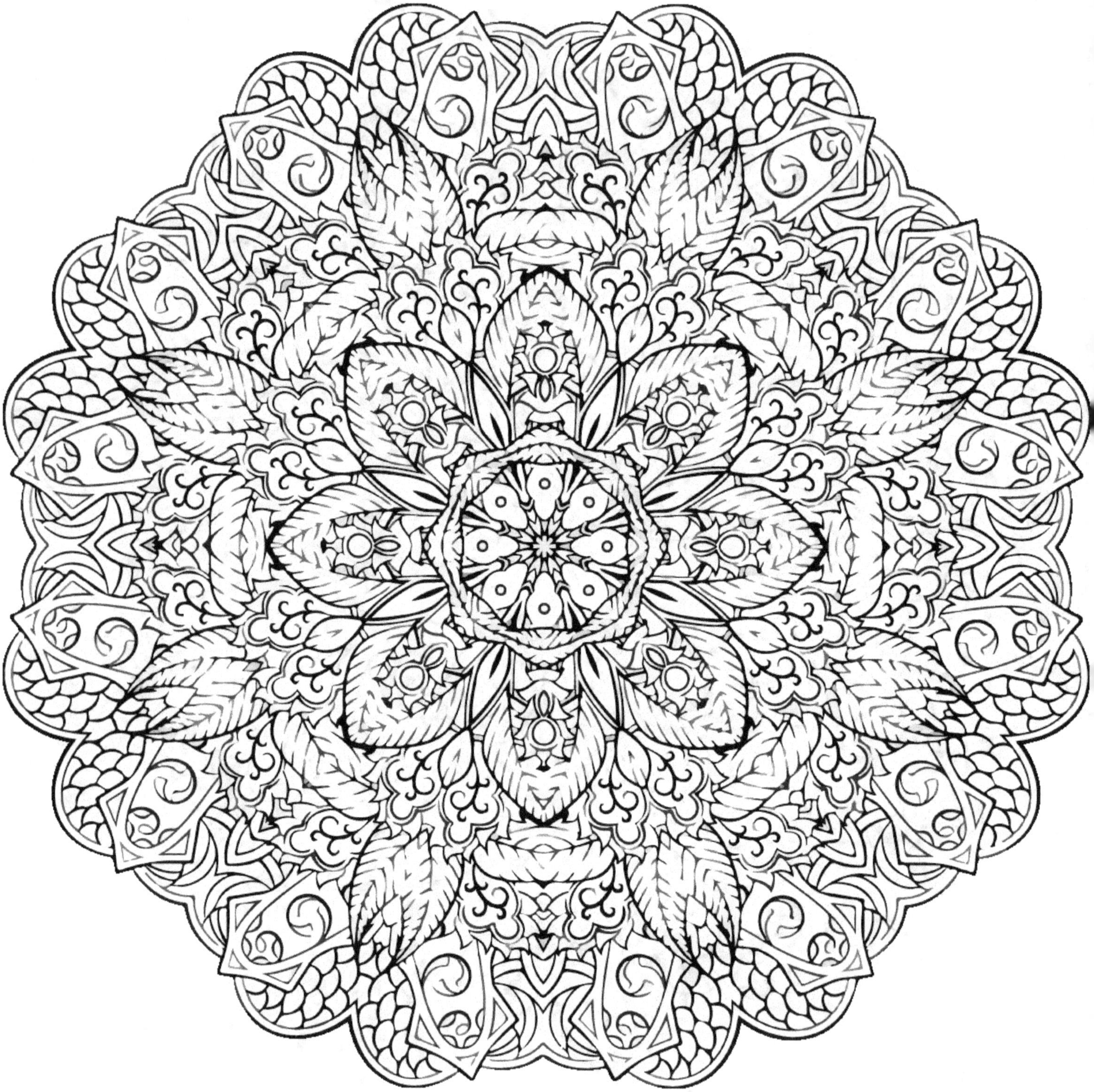

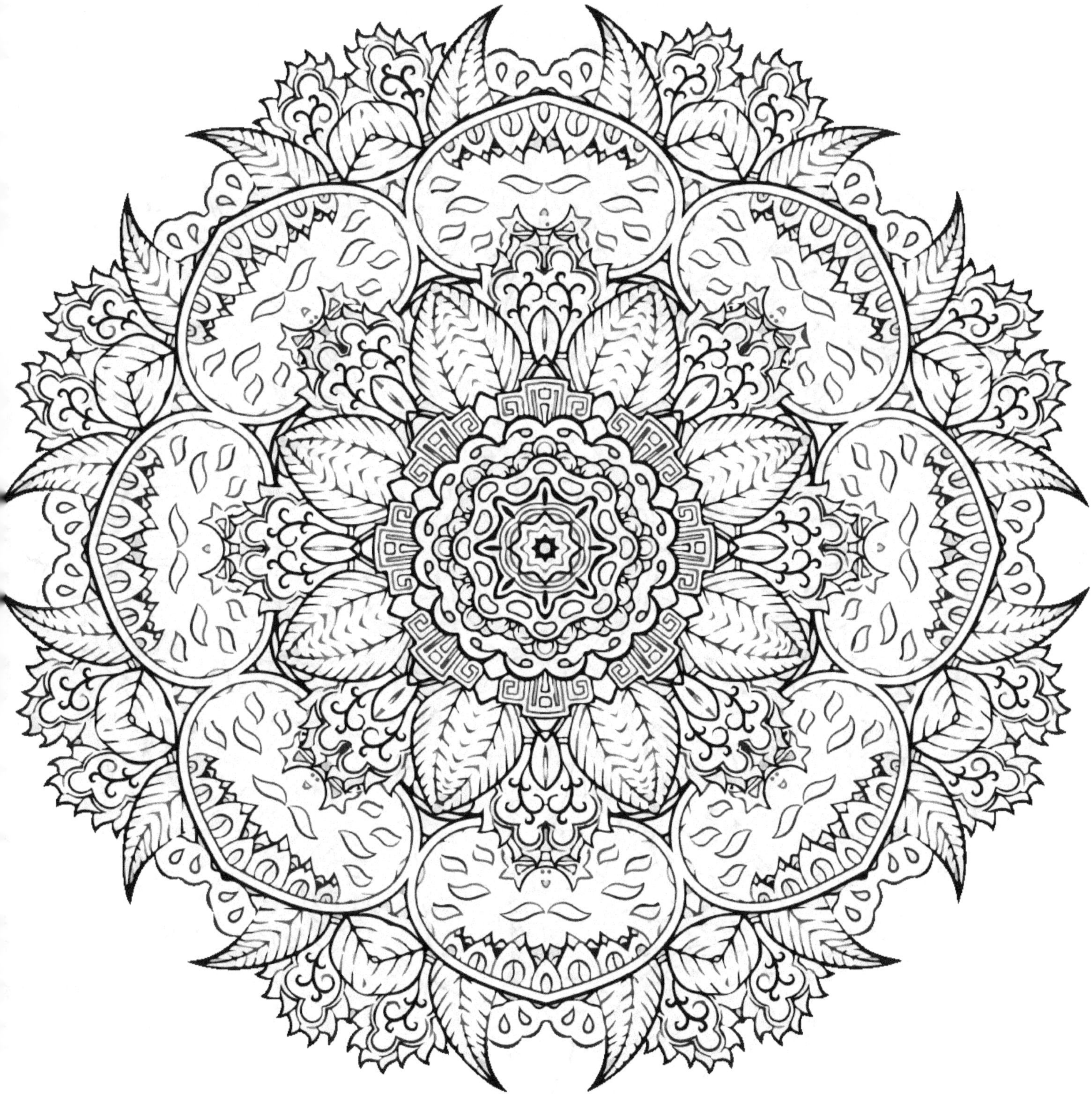

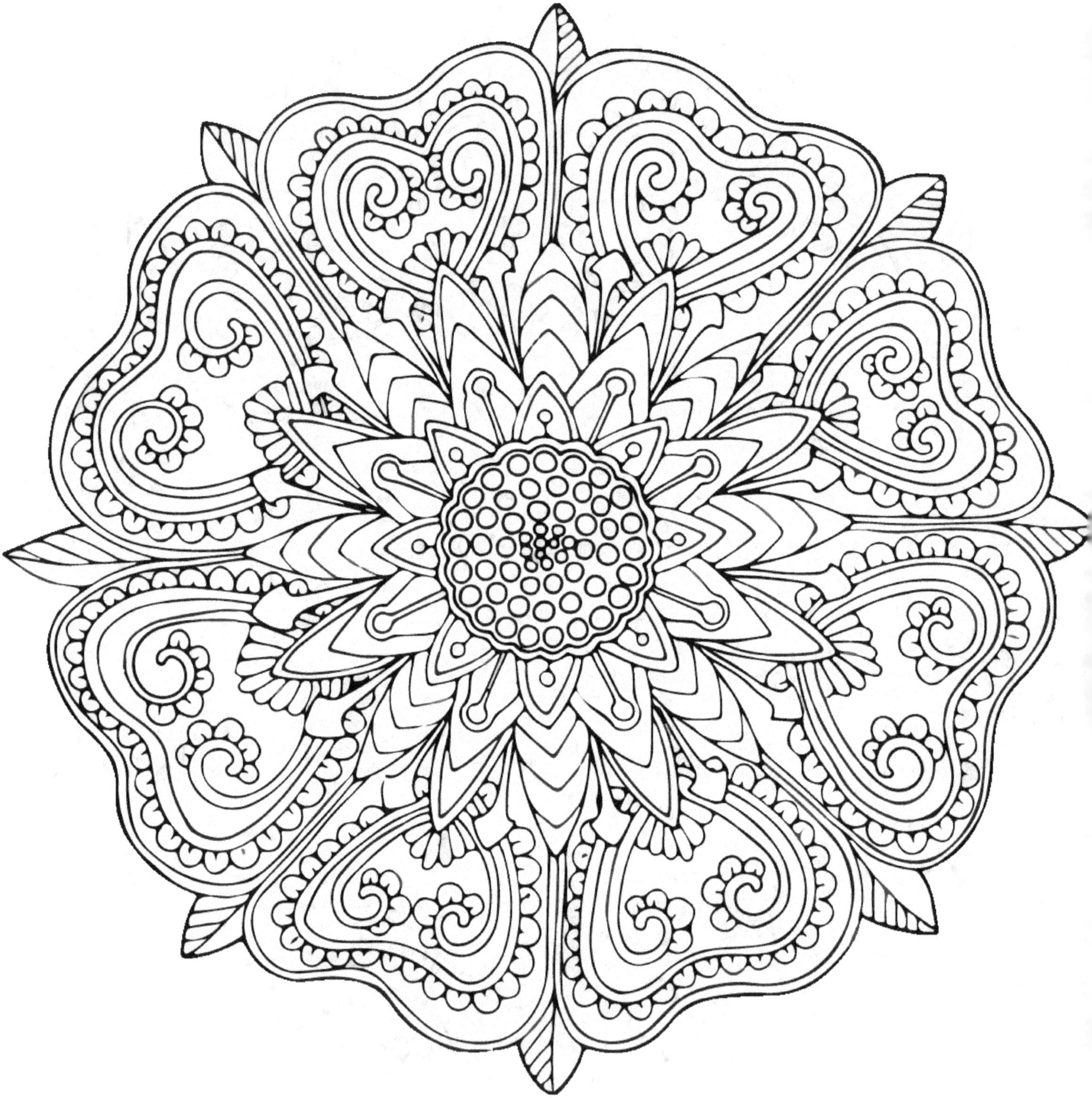

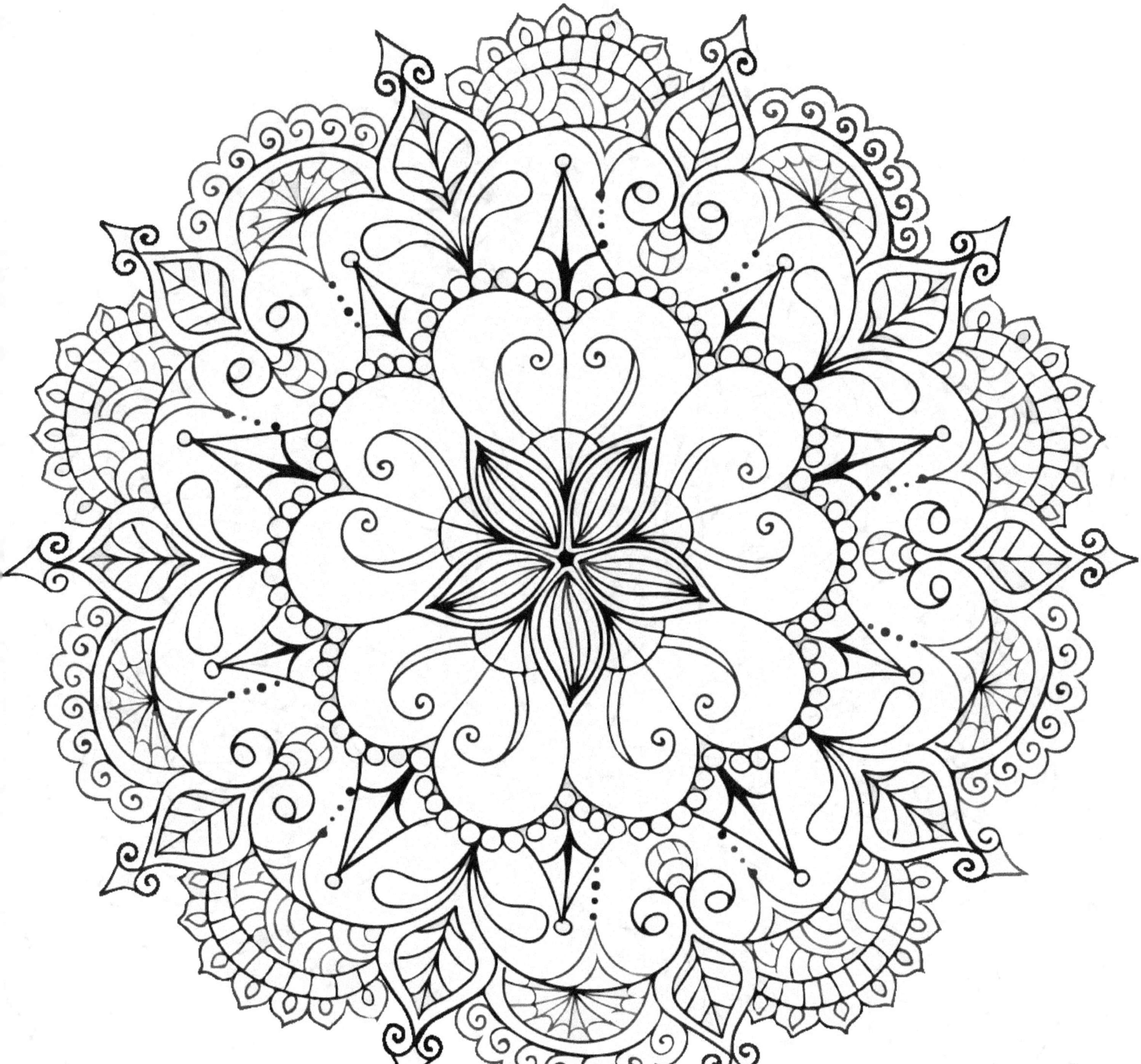

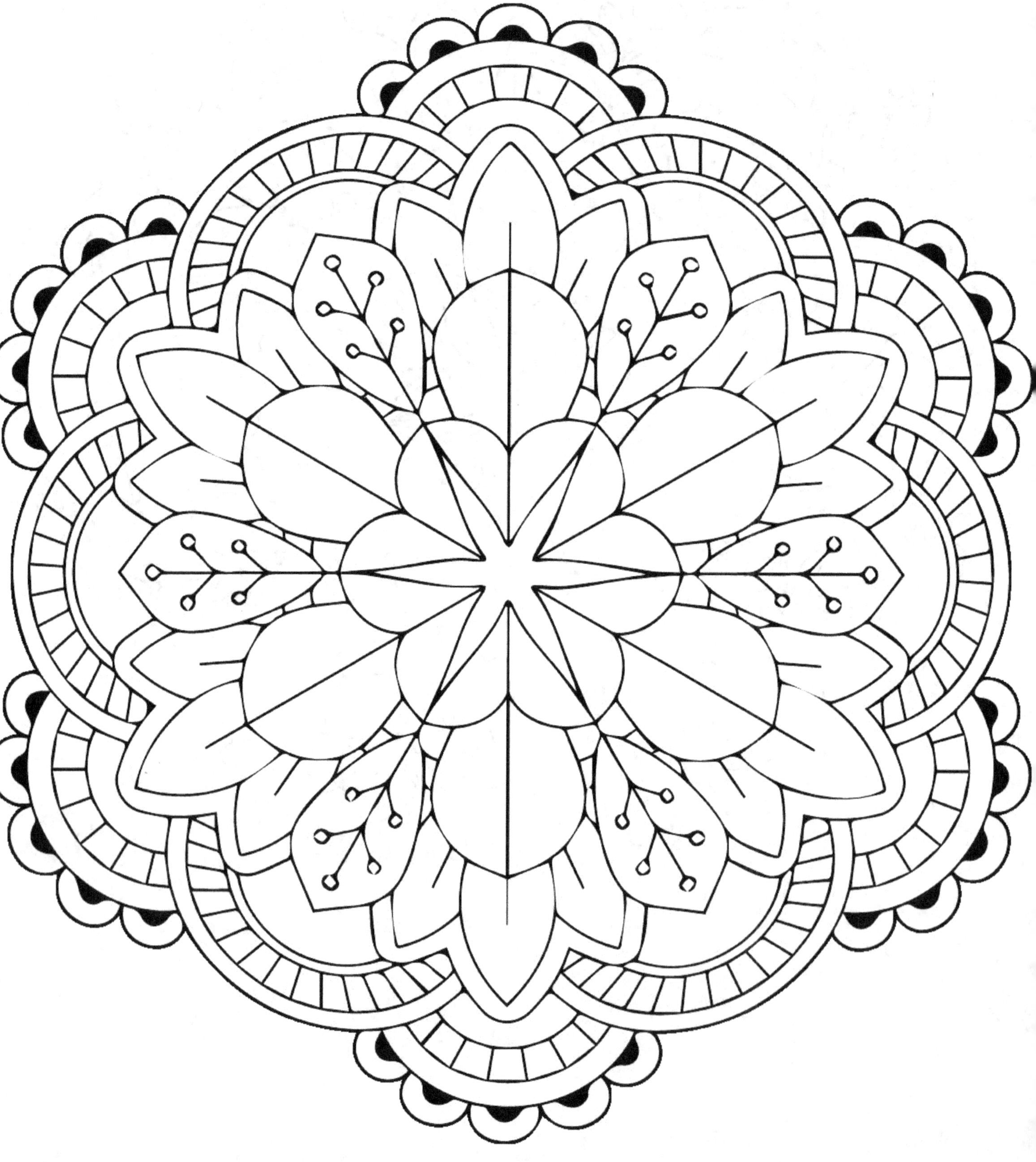

www.ingramcontent.com/pod-product-compliance
Lightning Source LLC
Chambersburg PA
CBHW080936220526
45465CB00008BA/3063
* 9 7 9 8 6 4 5 7 3 3 3 7 7 *